100 More
Easy Recipes
In Jars

Bonnie Scott

BONNIE SCOTT

ISBN-13: 978-1492936633

CONTENTS

100 More Easy Recipes in Jars

Jars, jars, jars – everyone is hooked on jars today for decorating, storing and organizing. Look at any homemaker blog, the shelves of your local craft store and the big box chain stores and you'll find tons of jars in every shape and size.

100 More Easy Recipes in Jars is the 2nd book in a series to incorporate this latest trend with a delicious homemade gift that's sure to please everyone.

You have an almost unlimited variety of choices when it comes to making gifts in jars. Even if you're not the greatest chef on the block, never fear. With this book you have a wealth of simple and easy recipes that will make your gift giving easy this year.

Whether you're looking for a recipe for a rich and decadent dessert, savory seasoning or warm, satisfying soup, you'll find a variety of recipes for almost any occasion in this latest collection. Use the easy-to-follow directions and add your own creative touch to create a fun and tasty gift. Make up a whole batch and you're ready for any last-minute gift-giving occasion that comes along.

These festive gift jars are great for a favorite teacher, your pastor or a thank-you gift for a helpful neighbor. You'll find many occasions that are just right for gifts in jars, so keep a few handy.

Filling the Jar

Whether you're using a Mason jar, glass canister or a plastic storage jar, make sure the inside of the jar stays clean as you fill it with your ingredients. You don't want a flour or powdered sugar coated jar on display, so wipe the inside as you add the layers if there is a mess on the glass.

Just like layered sand art, think about how you will position your layers. A variety in color, texture and thickness adds to the decorative look of your jar.

The contents will settle, so place the finest ground ingredients like flour in the bottom and work up to the coarsest items at the top if you are layering your jar.

Pack your layers to conserve space and create definite layers. Use a bean masher tool or a flat-bottomed glass to tamp down the layers. If you wind up with extra space at the top of the jar, add extra chocolate chips, nuts or other ingredients that are part of the recipe to fill the container to the top.

Fresh Ingredients

Don't even think about clearing out your pantry to make these gifts! Use only fresh ingredients, as the recipient may not use your recipe right away. Spices lose their flavor, nuts get rancid and items like baking soda and baking powder lose their potency.

Dry mixes will keep 6 to 8 months if stored in a cool, dry place sealed in jar until ready to use.

Some ingredients tend to harden when exposed to the air. Brown sugar is one culprit, and it's popular in many cookie and bar recipes. It's best to either inform the recipient that your recipe should be used within a few weeks or place the brown sugar in a sealed plastic bag.

Jar Sizes and Capacity

Here are the capacities of standard size canning jars:

Quart = 4 cups or 32 ounces

Pint = 2 cups or 16 ounces

Half pint = 1 cup or 8 ounces

Quarter pint = 1/2 cup or 4 ounces

If you are packing your ingredients tightly, you can fit:

Quart = 4 3/4 cups

Pint = 2 1/8 cups

Half pint = 1 cup + 2 tablespoons

Items like chocolate chips and nuts can't be compressed. If you're using some of these non-packable items and some packable items, the amount your jar will hold will probably fall in between the two amounts above.

Examples of Ball Jar Sizes

Half-Pint   Pint   Pint & a Half   Quart

Even Ball jars come in various shapes. For example, the pint size Ball jar comes in a squatty format or a tall shape.

You can purchase jars at your local grocery store, Wal-Mart, Target or craft stores. Most craft stores carry a large variety of jars; some jars have a one-piece lid that might be more convenient for storing the seasoning mixes in this book.

Visual Jar Filling

A canning funnel is inexpensive and will really help in filling the jars without making much of a mess inside the jar. Funnels can be found next to the canning jars in most stores.

The flour mixture is the best layer to put in the jar first because it will pack hard, and since it is so fine and dusty, by being first it won't get all over the chocolate chips or M&M's – layers you want to display cleanly.

Pack the flour layer well with a packing tool – bean masher like this one or the flat bottom of a glass.

Adding a layer like brown sugar creates layering interest for your jar masterpiece and at the same time, it holds the flour where it needs to remain. Measure the brown sugar, packed for the recipe, then unpack it to place it in the jar. Pack it again after it is in the jar.

After all the packable layers have been added, add the items that won't be packed, like chocolate chips, dried fruit and M&M's.

Hints and Tips

Some people think the jars are so pretty, they won't use them right away. If your jar contains brown sugar and the recipient decides to use the jar after a year, they will have to chisel the brown sugar out.

If the brown sugar does become hard in the jar, after removing it:

- Place the brown sugar in the microwave with a small container of water beside it. Microwave for one minute. Then, check and continue to microwave in 30-second increments until the sugar is soft.

The jars themselves are relatively inexpensive. A case of quart or pint jars is about $15 at Wal-Mart.

Use the small resealable snack bags (6 1/2" x 3 1/4") to add an ingredient to a jar if necessary, found at the Dollar Store.

Book one of *100 Easy Recipes in Jars* has 100 more recipes and 2000 additional labels and recipe cards for jars. Available in both Kindle and paperback versions.

Get Creative with Containers

Browse around a craft store, hobby store or department store like Wal-Mart or Target for loads of interesting containers to hold your gifts. Think outside the box and surprise your recipient with something for their home as well as for their tummy.

Kitchen utensils and accessories would be thoughtful add-ons for a newlywed couple or someone just starting out in their first apartment. Place your gift jar in a mixing bowl; add some utensils, measuring cups and tea towels for a perfect shower or housewarming gift.

Pack a teapot with ingredients to make almond tea bread or pecan coffee muffins. Add a box of a favorite tea and package it all together on a small serving tray.

Make a basket filled with movie night treats. Include the latest DVD, a jar of your homemade nuts or snacks, a couple packs of microwave popcorn and a container of vanilla hot chocolate. 100 Easy Recipes in Jars book one also has popcorn seasonings to add. Instead of a basket, use an oversized plastic bowl to use when the popcorn is ready to serve.

Seasoning Mixes

It is really quite cost-effective to make your own seasoning mixes. You can easily save 50% or more on spice mixes by making your own and it's a great way to get the taste you and your family prefer. You can also control the amount of ingredients like salt, MSG, preservatives, dyes and other additives.

Take a look at the spice and seasoning area of your local grocer. It seems that area is always expanding as new brands and flavor combinations keep adding to the number of spices and herbs on the shelves.

If you have a group of ethnic dishes that are always on your short list, create seasoning combinations to make preparing them a snap. Italian, Cajun or Mexican spice combos are ready when you are for quickly seasoning a favorite ethnic dish to perfection. Even everyday dishes like steamed veggies or microwave popcorn get an extra punch of flavor with your own personal style of flavoring.

Creating your own seasoning mixes is an easy way to indulge your creative culinary nature without spending hours bending over a hot stove. It's also far less costly to make up your own secret herb or seasoning recipes. You'll know they are fresh and you can make as much or as little as you choose.

By blending your own seasoning combinations, you can fine-tune each to suit your own taste of sweetness, heat and salt. Strong flavored or spicy seasonings can be tamed down or punched up to suit your family's taste buds. You can even have an adult and a kid-friendly version to please everyone.

To blend the seasonings together well, grind them in a spice or coffee grinder, food processor or use a mortar & pestle. This ensures that all the ingredients are the same size and well incorporated.

You can get great prices on large quantities of herbs and spices at wholesale stores like Costco, BJ's and Sam's Club. However, these are pretty big containers, so you probably should make up a bunch of these seasoning mixes for gifts. Remember, spices and herbs lose their potency rather quickly, so plan to use the spices within six months.

Fabric Jar Toppers

FABRIC PLACEMENT FOR USING 2 FABRICS

I normally use 2 pieces of fabric on the top of jars, but just one piece also works nicely. For 2 pieces, I use the placement above. For one fabric, just cut one square. For 2 different fabrics, cut 2 squares.

I use from a 4" square to a 9" square. Use a 6" or 6 1/2" square or even smaller if you want the top layer in a quart jar to be viewable. If the top portion of your quart jar is empty, you might make the squares larger to cover up the empty area. If the jar is a pint or half-pint, I would use a 4" square.

Use a thin brown rubber band about 3" long around the top of the jar over the fabric before adding the trim or ribbon. The rubber band will hold the fabric in place while you add the ribbon. Use approximately 30 inches of ribbon for each jar top.

Thin ribbons about 3/8" work well as ribbons thinner than 3/8". Although if the ribbon is too thin, the rubber band may show through. Also wider ribbon that is translucent and light will work. I have used ribbons like that in this book that are 1 1/2" wide and 1" wide. The ribbon below is 1 1/2" wide.

All the ribbons, trim and fabrics used in this book are available at either Hobby Lobby or Joann Fabric stores.

Labels, Hang Tags, Recipe Cards

Use the labels and more available at www.NorthPoleChristmas.com/jarsbook2.html

There are at least 2 pages of labels specifically for each recipe in separate pdf files available to print. They can be printed on paper, 2 1/2" white round labels or 2 1/2" round Kraft Brown labels.

The Kraft Brown labels (by Avery) produce a more subdued look to the label because the colors on top of brown won't be as vibrant as the white labels. Some of the labels in the photos in this book were made with the Kraft Brown labels. Use the following Avery labels for these templates:

Avery Kraft Brown 2 1/2" labels #22818

Avery Glossy White 2 1/2" labels #41462

If you don't want to use labels, printing the jar labels on good quality paper works just as well. Cut them out and stick the labels to your jars with double-faced tape.

Since there are 100 recipes in this book and at least 2 pages of labels per recipe, making over 200 pages of labels, there are way too many to include in this book. So the labels are available on the internet and can be accessed with your computer and printed. There is a Google+ page listed on www.NorthPoleChristmas.com/jarsbook2.html that you can post questions for me to answer, if need be.

JAR LAYERS

The Jar Layers section includes ingredients that will be layered in jars and the recipient does the actual cooking using the attached recipe.

BREAD

Sweet Cornbread Muffins

FILLS ONE QUART GLASS JAR

2 cups all-purpose flour
1 1/2 cups yellow cornmeal
1/2 cup + 2 tablespoons sugar
3 tablespoons baking powder
3/4 teaspoon salt

Combine all ingredients and place in a quart jar. Seal jar.

Attach the following recipe to the jar:

Sweet Cornbread Muffins

2 tablespoons vegetable oil
1/3 cup milk
1 egg
1 cup cornbread mix from jar

Preheat oven to 400 degrees F. In a medium bowl, combine oil, milk and egg. Add 1 cup of cornbread mix from jar and mix well. Spray an 8x8-inch baking pan or 6 muffin cups with non-stick cooking spray. Pour batter into pan or muffin cups. (Fill muffin cups 2/3 full.) Bake at 400 degrees F for 15 to 17 minutes. Yield: 6 muffins.

Almond Tea Bread

FILLS ONE QUART GLASS JAR

2 cups flour
1/4 teaspoon baking powder
1/4 teaspoon baking soda
1/4 teaspoon salt
1 cup sugar
1/2 cup slivered almonds

Mix together flour, baking powder, baking soda and salt in a bowl. Layer in quart jar, packing well after each layer: flour mixture then sugar. Place almonds on top.
Seal jar.

Attach the following recipe to the jar:

Almond Tea Bread

1/2 cup butter, softened
1 egg
1/2 cup evaporated milk
1/4 teaspoon almond extract

In a bowl, combine butter, egg, milk and almond extract. Add the contents of the jar and mix well. Pour batter into a greased 9 x 5 loaf pan. Bake at 350 degrees for 1 hour. Cool before serving. Yield: 1 loaf.

Pumpkin Bread

FILLS ONE QUART GLASS JAR

1 3/4 cups flour
1 teaspoon baking soda
1 teaspoon nutmeg
1 teaspoon cinnamon
3/4 teaspoon salt
1/2 teaspoon baking powder
1/2 teaspoon allspice
1/4 teaspoon ground cloves
1 1/2 cups sugar
1/2 cup pecans, chopped

In a bowl, combine flour, baking soda, nutmeg, cinnamon, salt, baking powder, allspice, and cloves. Place flour mixture in a quart jar, then sugar, packing each layer. Add nuts on top. Seal jar.

Attach the following recipe to the jar:

Pumpkin Bread
1/3 cup water
1/2 vegetable cup oil
2 eggs, beaten
1 cup pumpkin puree

Preheat oven to 350 degrees F. Grease a 9x5-inch loaf pan. Pour contents of jar in a large bowl. Stir in water and oil. Beat eggs and mix into batter. Blend in the pumpkin. Pour batter into loaf pan. Bake for 1 hour or until passes toothpick test. Cool 5 minutes in pan before removing. Yield: 1 loaf.

Banana Nut Bread

FILLS ONE QUART GLASS JAR

2 cups flour
1/8 teaspoon salt
1 teaspoon baking soda
1/2 teaspoon baking powder
1 cup sugar
1/2 cup chopped nuts

Mix together flour, salt, baking soda and baking powder in a bowl. Layer in quart jar, packing well: flour mixture, sugar, then add nuts on top. Seal jar.

Attach the following recipe to the jar:

Banana Nut Bread

3 bananas
1/2 cup oil
2 eggs, beaten
3 tablespoons milk
1/2 teaspoon vanilla

In a large bowl, mash 3 bananas. Add oil, eggs, milk and vanilla; mix well. Pour the contents of the jar into the bowl and beat well. Pour into a greased and floured loaf pan and bake at 350 degrees F for 1 hour. Yield: 1 loaf.

Raisin Bread

FILLS ONE QUART GLASS JAR

3 cups all-purpose flour
3 teaspoons baking powder
2 teaspoons ground cinnamon
1 teaspoon salt
1/2 teaspoon baking soda
1/2 cup white sugar
1 1/4 cup raisins

In a bowl, combine flour, baking powder, cinnamon, salt and baking soda. Place flour mixture in quart jar, then sugar, packing each layer. Place raisins in a small resealable plastic bag and add to jar on top of sugar. Seal jar.

Attach the following recipe to the jar:

Raisin Bread

1 egg
1/4 cup butter, melted
1/2 cup applesauce
1 cup milk

Preheat oven to 350 degrees F. Grease a 9x5x3 inch loaf pan. Pour the contents of the jar in a large bowl. Make a well in the center. In another bowl, beat egg, mix in butter, applesauce and milk. Pour into well. Stir just enough to moisten. Pour into loaf pan.

Bake at 350 degrees F for 55 to 60 minutes. Yield: 1 loaf.

Lemon Nut Bread

FILLS ONE QUART GLASS JAR

1 1/2 cups all-purpose flour
1/2 teaspoon salt
1 teaspoon baking powder
1 cup white sugar
1/2 cup chopped walnuts

In a bowl, combine flour, salt and baking powder. Place flour mixture in quart jar, then sugar, packing each layer. Add nuts on top. Seal jar.

Attach the following recipe to the jar:

Lemon Nut Bread

6 tablespoons butter, melted
2 eggs
1/2 cup milk
1 teaspoon lemon zest

Glaze:
1/2 cup white sugar
1 lemon, juiced

In a large bowl, mix butter and eggs together. Add milk and contents of jar; mix well. Stir in grated lemon zest. Pour batter in a greased and floured 9x5-inch loaf pan. Bake at 350 degrees F for 1 hour. Allow bread to cool in the pan for 5 minutes.

Glaze:

Combine sugar and the juice of a lemon. Remove bread from pan. Pour glaze over warm bread.

Cherry Bread

FILLS ONE QUART GLASS JAR

1 1/2 cups flour
1 1/2 teaspoons baking powder
1 cup sugar
3/4 cup nuts, chopped

Mix flour and baking powder. Place flour mixture in jar, then sugar, packing each layer. Add nuts on top. Seal jar.

Attach the following recipe to the jar:

Cherry Bread

2 eggs, well beaten
1 5 ounce jar maraschino cherries cut up – juice and all

In a large bowl, combine the eggs and cherries with cherry juice. Add the contents of the jar and mix well. Bake in a well-greased 9 x 5 inch pan at 350 degrees F for 1 hour.

Yield: 1 loaf.

BARS

Deep Dish Brownies

FILLS ONE PINT GLASS JAR

This recipe makes brownies that taste like store-bought prepared mixes ... only richer! It gets an A+ all around for taste and ease of cooking.

3/4 cup flour
1/2 teaspoon baking powder
1/2 teaspoon salt
1/2 cup cocoa
1 cup sugar

Mix together flour, baking powder and salt in a bowl. Layer in pint jar: flour mixture, cocoa, sugar. Pack well after each layer. Seal jar.

Attach the following recipe to the jar:

Deep Dish Brownies

3/4 cup butter, melted
1 1/2 teaspoons vanilla
1/2 cup sugar
3 eggs

Preheat oven to 350 degrees F. Blend melted butter, vanilla and sugar in a mixing bowl. Add the eggs, beat well with a spoon. Gradually add contents of jar to egg mixture and stir until blended well. Spread in greased 8" square pan. Bake at 350 degrees F for 40 minutes. Cool and cut into squares.

Chewy Butterscotch Brownies

FILLS ONE QUART GLASS JAR

1 1/4 cups all-purpose flour
1/2 teaspoon baking powder
1/4 teaspoon salt
1 cup brown sugar, packed
3/4 cup butterscotch-flavored morsels
1/2 cup pecans or walnuts, chopped
plus
1 cup butterscotch-flavored morsels for frosting

Mix the flour, baking powder and salt together in a bowl. Place the flour mixture in a jar, pack. Then add the brown sugar and pack. Add 3/4 cup butterscotch morsels, then the nuts, then the remaining butterscotch morsels on top. (Be sure to put the butterscotch morsels for the frosting on top, so they can be removed from the jar easily by the recipient.) Seal jar.

Attach the following recipe to the jar:

Frosted Butterscotch Brownies

1/2 cup butter, softened
1 tablespoon vanilla extract
2 eggs

Preheat oven to 350 degrees F. Remove the top layer of butterscotch-flavored morsels from the jar (down to the nuts) and set aside. These will be used for frosting.

Mix the butter and vanilla extract in a large bowl until creamy. Add the eggs and beat well. Pour the remainder of the jar contents into the bowl and mix until well blended. Pour the mixture into a lightly greased 13x9 inch baking pan. Bake for 30 minutes or until inserted toothpick comes out clean.

Frosting - Butterscotch Glaze:

3/4 cup butterscotch-flavored morsels (from jar)
2 tablespoons water
2 tablespoons sugar
1 1/2 teaspoons light corn syrup

Bring corn syrup, water and sugar to a boil in a pan over medium-high heat. Remove from heat and add the reserved butterscotch-flavored chips. Stir until all chips are melted. Pour glaze over brownies and spread evenly. Let cool before cutting.

Dual Chip Bars

FILLS ONE QUART GLASS JAR

1 1/2 cups graham cracker crumbs (about 24 squares)
2 cups semisweet chocolate chips
1 cup peanut butter chips

Place the graham cracker crumbs in a small resealable plastic bag. In a quart jar, place the chocolate chips and peanut butter chips. Add the bag of graham crackers on top. Seal jar.

Attach the following recipe to the jar:

Dual Chip Bars

1/2 cup butter
1 can (14 oz.) sweetened condensed milk

Preheat oven to 350 degrees F. Put butter in a 13x9x2-inch baking pan; place pan in oven until melted. Remove from oven.

Remove graham cracker crumbs from jar and sprinkle crumbs evenly over butter. Pour milk uniformly over crumbs. Sprinkle the remaining contents of jar over milk; press down firmly. Bake at 350 degrees F for 25 to 30 minutes or until golden brown. Cool on a wire rack before cutting.

Easy Chocolate Brownies

FILLS ONE QUART GLASS JAR

2 cups biscuit baking mix
1 cup coarsely chopped nuts
1 (12 oz.) pkg. semi-sweet chocolate chips

Pack the biscuit mix, nuts and chocolate chips in a quart jar. Be sure to put chocolate chips on top so 1 cup of the chocolate can be removed easily. (Or put 1 cup of the chocolate chips in a small resealable plastic bag and label as 1 cup.) Seal jar.

Attach the following recipe to the jar:

Easy Chocolate Brownies

1/4 cup margarine
1 (14 oz.) can sweetened condensed milk
1 egg, beaten
1 teaspoon vanilla
Powdered sugar

Preheat oven to 350 degrees F. Remove 1 cup of chocolate chips from jar. In a large saucepan over low heat, melt margarine and 1 cup chocolate chips from the jar together; remove from heat. Add milk, egg, vanilla and remainder of ingredients from the jar.

Pour into well-greased 13x9" baking pan. Bake 20 to 25 minutes or until brownies begin to pull away from sides of pan. Cool. Sprinkle with powdered sugar. Yield: 2 dozen.

Peanut Butter Chocolate Bars

FILLS ONE QUART GLASS JAR

1 cup flour
1/4 teaspoon salt
1 1/4 cups sugar
1 (11 oz.) pkg. chocolate chips

Mix flour and salt together. Put flour mixture in jar and pack. Add sugar, then chocolate chips. (Place chocolate chips on top so the recipient can remove 3/4 cup easily.) Seal jar.

Attach the following recipe to the jar:

Peanut Butter Chocolate Bars

1 cup peanut butter
6 tablespoons butter, softened
3 eggs
1 teaspoon vanilla

Preheat oven to 350 degrees F. Remove 3/4 cup of chocolate chips from jar; set aside. In large bowl, beat butter and peanut butter until smooth, about 1 minute. Add eggs and vanilla; beat until well mixed and creamy. Mix in remaining contents of jar.

Spread in an ungreased 13x9" pan. Bake at 350 degrees F 25 to 30 minutes or until edges begin to turn brown. Remove from oven and immediately sprinkle remaining chocolate chips over cookie layer. Let stand 5 minutes; spread chocolate evenly over top. Cut into bars.

Chewy Granola Bars

FILLS ONE QUART GLASS JAR

2/3 cup brown sugar
2 cups quick oats
1/4 cup wheat germ
1/3 cup sunflower seeds
2/3 cup nuts, chopped
1/3 cup raisins or dried cherries

Layer in order listed in a quart jar, packing the first 3 layers well. Raisins or cherries can be put in a resealable plastic bag (to preserve freshness) and added on top of nuts. Seal jar.

Attach the following recipe to the jar:

Chewy Granola Bars

1/3 cup butter, melted
1/3 cup light corn syrup
1/2 cup peanut butter
2 teaspoons vanilla

Preheat oven to 350 degrees F. In a large bowl, mix the butter, corn syrup, peanut butter and vanilla together. Add contents of jar and mix well. Press into an 8x8-inch or 9x9-inch pan. Bake at 350 degrees F for 15 to 20 minutes.

Egg-Less Cocoa Crazy Cake

FILLS ONE QUART GLASS JAR

1 3/4 cups flour
1 teaspoon baking soda
1/4 teaspoon salt
1 cup sugar
3 tablespoons unsweetened cocoa

Mix flour, baking soda and salt together. Put flour mixture in jar and pack. Mix sugar and cocoa together. Add sugar mixture to jar and pack. Seal jar.

Attach the following recipe to the jar:

Egg-Less Cocoa Crazy Cake

1 teaspoon vanilla
1 tablespoon vinegar
5 tablespoons butter, melted
1 cup water
Powdered sugar (optional)

Pour the contents of the jar into a bowl. Make 3 wells in the dry ingredients. Pour the vanilla in 1 well, the vinegar in another, and the melted butter in the third. Pour the water over all and beat with a spoon until well blended. Pour into greased 9" square pan and bake at 350 degrees F for 25 minutes. When cool, sprinkle with powdered sugar or frost.

S'more Brownies

FILLS ONE QUART GLASS JAR

Be sure to use the small plastic snack bags for packing so they all fit in the jar. I used a quart jar in a different shape than a regular quart canning jar so it was easier to pack the jar with the plastic bags without disturbing the flour and other ingredients.

1/2 cup and 2 tablespoons all-purpose flour
1/2 teaspoon baking powder
1/2 teaspoon salt
1/3 cup unsweetened cocoa powder
1 cup and 2 tablespoons sugar
2 graham crackers
3 (1.5 oz.) milk chocolate bars
3/4 cup miniature marshmallows
3 small resealable snack bags (6 1/2" x 3 1/4")

Combine flour, baking powder and salt. Put in quart jar and pack firmly. Add cocoa powder as the next layer and pack. Add sugar and pack firmly.

Break the graham crackers into small pieces and place in a small resealable snack bag. Break each chocolate bar into about 16 pieces and place in another snack bag. In the final snack bag, add the marshmallows. Squeeze as much air as possible out of each snack bag.

Cut a double layer of wax paper to fit inside the jar and lay it on top of the last sugar layer. Now add the graham cracker bag, chocolate bag and marshmallow bag to the jar. Seal jar.

Attach the following recipe to the jar:

S'more Brownies

6 tablespoons butter or margarine
2 eggs, slightly beaten

Preheat oven to 350 degrees F. Remove the 3 plastic bags from inside the jar and set aside. Remove the wax paper from the jar and empty the ingredients of the jar into a large bowl. Add the butter or margarine and eggs. Mix until well blended.

Spray an 8" or 9" square baking dish with non-stick cooking spray. Pour batter into pan and spread evenly. Bake at 350 degrees F. for 20 minutes. Remove, sprinkle the contents of each plastic bag on top of the brownie and bake for 10 minutes more. Allow to cool before cutting into squares.

Noel Bars

FILLS ONE PINT GLASS JAR

1/3 cup flour
1/8 teaspoon baking soda
1/8 teaspoon salt
1 cup brown sugar
1/2 to 3/4 cup chopped nuts

Combine flour, salt and baking soda in bowl. Put in jar and pack. Add brown sugar and pack. Add nuts on top. Seal jar.

Attach the following recipe to the jar:

Noel Bars

2 tablespoons butter
2 eggs, beaten
1 teaspoon vanilla
Powdered sugar
Green icing

Preheat oven to 350 degrees F. Melt butter in 9x9x2inch pan. Pour contents of jar in a bowl. Add eggs and vanilla; mix well. Carefully pour batter over butter in pan. Do not stir.

Bake at 350 degrees F for 20 to 25 minutes. Remove from oven and sprinkle with powdered sugar. Invert onto wax paper on a rack immediately. When cool, cut into long bars and write "Noel" in green icing on powdered sugar side.

Double Chocolate Cupcakes

FILLS ONE QUART GLASS JAR

Fit these ingredients into a quart jar and there will be enough room at the top of the jar to add some cupcake liners.

1 1/2 cups flour
1/2 cup sugar
1/4 cup unsweetened cocoa
1 teaspoon baking soda
1/2 teaspoon salt
1/3 cup semi-sweet chocolate mini morsels

Combine flour, sugar, cocoa, baking soda and salt in a medium bowl. Put in quart jar and pack firmly. Add chocolate mini morsels on top. Seal jar. *(Note: There really isn't enough quantity-wise of the sugar and cocoa to make a layer that will show, so just mix all the ingredients together.)*

Attach the following recipe to the jar:

Double Chocolate Cupcakes

1/2 cup unsweetened orange juice
1/3 cup water
3 tablespoons vegetable oil
1 tablespoon vinegar
1 teaspoon vanilla
1 teaspoon powdered sugar

Pour the contents of the jar in a bowl; make a well in center.

Combine orange juice, water, oil, vinegar, and vanilla; add to dry ingredients, stirring until just moistened.

Pour batter in muffin pans lined with cupcake liners, filling 2/3 full. Bake at 375 degrees F for 12 minutes or until a toothpick inserted in center comes out clean. Remove from pans and cool on rack. Sprinkle with powdered sugar. Yield: 12 servings.

Ginger Spice Muffins

FILLS ONE QUART GLASS JAR

3 1/2 cups flour
1/4 cup sugar
2 tablespoons baking powder
1 teaspoon baking soda
2 teaspoons ground cinnamon
1 teaspoon ground nutmeg
1/2 teaspoon ground ginger
1/2 teaspoon ground cloves
1 teaspoon salt

Combine all the ingredients in a bowl. Put in quart jar; pack well. Seal jar.

Attach the following recipe to the jar:

Ginger Spice Muffins

1/2 cup butter or margarine, melted
2 eggs
2 teaspoons vanilla
2 cups milk

Preheat oven to 400 degrees F. Grease 24 muffin tins or use paper liners. In a large bowl, mix butter, eggs, vanilla and milk, then add the contents of the jar. Stir the mixture just until the ingredients are well mixed; batter will be lumpy. Pour into muffin pans, filling 2/3 full and bake for 15 minutes at 400 degrees F. Yield: 2 dozen.

Pecan Coffee Muffins

FILLS ONE QUART GLASS JAR

1 cup pecans
1 3/4 cups flour
1/4 teaspoon salt
3 teaspoons baking powder
1/2 cup dark brown sugar, firmly packed

Coarsely chop pecans. In a large bowl, combine flour, salt and baking powder. Put flour mixture in quart jar, then brown sugar, packing each layer. Add pecans on top. Seal jar.

Attach the following recipe to the jar:

Pecan Coffee Muffins

1 egg
1/2 cup milk
1/2 cup butter, melted
2 teaspoons strong cold coffee
1 teaspoon vanilla

Line 12 muffin cups with cupcake liners or spray lightly with non-stick cooking spray. In a large bowl, lightly beat egg. Add milk, butter, coffee and vanilla to the egg; blend well. Add the contents of the jar; mix just until combined. Spoon mixture into buttered muffin cups. Bake at 400 degrees F for 16 to 20 minutes or until inserted toothpick comes out clean. Yield: 12 muffins.

Crumb Muffins

FILLS ONE QUART GLASS JAR

1 1/2 cups flour
1 teaspoon baking powder
1 teaspoon baking soda
1/2 teaspoon salt
3/4 cup white sugar

Crumb topping:
1/3 cup packed brown sugar
2 tablespoons all-purpose flour
1/8 teaspoon ground cinnamon

Combine flour, baking powder, baking soda and salt in a bowl. Put in quart jar; pack. Add white sugar on top and pack. Mix the crumb topping ingredients together and place in a resealable small plastic bag; label the bag. Put on top in quart jar. Seal jar.

Attach the following recipe to the jar:

Crumb Muffins

3 bananas, mashed
1 egg, lightly beaten
1/3 cup butter, melted

1 tablespoon butter, softened

Preheat oven to 375 degrees F. Line ten muffin cups with cupcake liners or spray lightly with non-stick cooking spray. Remove the bag from the top of the jar; set aside.

In a large bowl, beat together bananas, egg and melted butter. Add the contents of the jar (except for topping in bag) and stir just until combined well. Fill muffin cups 2/3 full with batter.

Bake at 375 degrees F for 18 to 20 minutes or until a toothpick inserted comes out clean.

Topping:

In a small bowl, pour contents of topping bag. Mix in 1 tablespoon softened butter until well mixed. Sprinkle mixture on top of muffins.

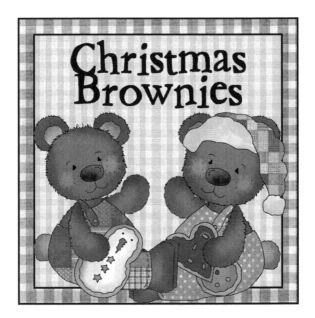

Brownies in a Jar

FILLS ONE QUART GLASS JAR

1 cup all-purpose flour
1/2 teaspoon baking powder
1/4 teaspoon salt
1 1/2 cups sugar
1/3 cups Hershey's unsweetened cocoa
1/2 cups mini semi-sweet chocolate chips
1 cup peanut butter chips or white chocolate chips

Mix flour, baking powder and salt together. Put flour mixture in a quart jar and pack. Mix sugar and cocoa together. Add sugar mixture to jar and pack. Add mini chocolate chips next, then peanut butter or white chips. Seal jar.

Attach the following recipe to the jar:

Brownies

1/2 cup butter, softened
2 eggs, slightly beaten

Preheat oven to 350 degrees F. Empty brownie mix from jar into a large bowl. Add butter and eggs. Gently stir to combine. Spread in a greased and floured 8-inch square baking pan. Bake at 350 degrees F for 35 minutes. Cool in pan. Cut into bars.

COOKIES & CANDY

Most of the cookie recipes yield about 24 cookies, give or take a few depending on the ingredients in the jar and the size of the cookie.

Christmas Cookies

FILLS ONE QUART GLASS JAR

This recipe can also be cut in half and put into pint jars. Regular Rice Krispies and chocolate chips or other flavor chips, like peanut butter, may be used in place of Cocoa Krispies and white chocolate chips.

1 1/2 cups all-purpose flour
3/4 teaspoon baking soda
1/4 teaspoon baking powder
1/4 cup sugar
1/2 cup packed brown sugar
1/2 cup rolled oats (also called old fashioned oats)
1/2 cup red & green M&M's
1/2 cup cocoa crisped-rice cereal
1/2 cup white chocolate chips

In a bowl, combine the flour, baking soda and baking powder. Layer in quart jar in this order: flour mixture, sugar, brown sugar and rolled oats. Pack well after each layer. On top of packed layers, lay M&M's, cereal and chocolate chips. Seal jar.

Attach the following recipe to the jar:

Christmas Cookies

1/2 cup butter
1/2 teaspoon vanilla extract
1 egg

Cream butter, vanilla and egg in a large bowl. Add the contents of the jar and stir until well blended (expect the mix to be dry, but add a few tablespoons of water, if necessary, to combine). Drop by rounded tablespoons on an ungreased baking sheet. Bake at 350 degrees for 10 to 12 minutes.

Cranberry White Chocolate Cookies

FILLS ONE QUART GLASS JAR

1 + 1/8 cups all-purpose flour
1/2 teaspoon salt
1/2 teaspoon baking soda
1/3 cup brown sugar, packed
1/3 cup white sugar
1/2 cup rolled oats
1/2 cup dried cranberries
1/2 cup vanilla flavored baking chips
1/2 cup chopped pecans

In a bowl, mix flour, salt and baking soda. In a quart jar, layer ingredients in this order: flour mixture, brown sugar, white sugar, and oats, packing firmly after adding each layer. Place the cranberries, baking chips and pecans on top. Seal jar.

Attach the following recipe to the jar:

Cranberry White Chocolate Chip Cookies

1/2 cup softened butter
1 egg
1 teaspoon vanilla

Preheat oven to 350 degrees F. Grease a baking sheet or line with parchment paper. In a bowl, beat together butter, egg and vanilla until creamy. Add the contents of jar and stir by hand until well mixed. Drop by heaping spoonful on a baking sheet, about 2 inches apart. Bake at 350 degrees F 8 to 10 minutes. Yield: 18 cookies.

Cocoa Peanut Butter Cookie Mix

FILLS ONE QUART GLASS JAR

Clean the inside of the jar with a dry paper towel after adding the confectioners' sugar.

1 1/2 cups all-purpose flour
1 teaspoon baking powder
1/4 teaspoon salt
1 cup packed brown sugar
1 1/2 cups confectioners' sugar
3/4 cups cocoa powder

In a bowl, mix together flour, baking powder and salt. Layer ingredients in a quart jar in this order: flour mixture, brown sugar, confectioners' sugar and cocoa powder. Pack each layer firmly because it will be a tight fit. Seal jar.

Attach the following recipe to the jar:

Cocoa Peanut Butter Cookies

1/2 cup butter, softened
1/2 cup creamy peanut butter
1 egg, slightly beaten
1 teaspoon vanilla

Empty the contents of the jar into a large bowl and mix well. Add butter, peanut butter, egg and vanilla to the bowl. Mix until well blended. Form into 1 1/4 inch balls and place a few inches apart on a parchment lined baking sheet. Press each cookie down with a fork. Bake at 350 degrees F for 9 to 11 minutes, until edges are browned. Cool 5 minutes on baking sheet, then transfer to a cooling rack to finish cooling. Yield: 3 dozen cookies.

Orange Cookie Mix

FILLS ONE QUART GLASS JAR

1 3/4 cups flour
1/2 teaspoon baking soda
1/2 teaspoon baking powder
1/2 cup Tang orange powdered drink mix
3/4 cup sugar
1 1/2 cups vanilla flavored baking chips

In a bowl, mix flour, baking soda and baking powder. In a quart jar, layer ingredients in this order: flour mixture, Tang and sugar. Pack firmly after each addition. Lay the baking chips on top. Seal jar.

Attach the following recipe to the jar:

Orange Cookies

1/2 cup butter or margarine, softened
1 egg
1 teaspoon vanilla

Pour the contents of the jar into a bowl; mix well. Add butter, egg and vanilla; stir until well blended. Shape into one inch balls. Bake at 375 degrees F for 12 to 13 minutes, until tops are lightly browned. Yield: 2 1/2 dozen.

Chocolate Reindeer Droppings

FILLS ONE QUART GLASS JAR

2/3 cup coconut
2 cups quick oats
1 1/3 cups sugar
1/4 cup cocoa

Place in jar in this order: coconut, quick oats, sugar, cocoa. It may be easier for removal if the sugar and cocoa are placed in resealable small plastic bags and added to the top of the jar. Seal jar.

Attach the following recipe to the jar:

Chocolate Reindeer Droppings

1/3 cup milk
1/3 cup butter

In a pan, boil milk, butter, and from the jar - cocoa and sugar. Remove from heat and add in the remainder of the jar ingredients. Mix well and drop by spoonful on wax paper. Refrigerate.

Chocolate Walnut Cookies

FILLS ONE QUART GLASS JAR

1 cup flour
1/2 teaspoon baking powder
1 teaspoon salt
1 cup sugar
1 cup chopped walnuts
3 squares unsweetened chocolate

Mix together flour, baking powder and salt in a bowl. Layer in quart jar: flour mixture, sugar, walnuts. Pack well after each layer. Add the 3 squares of chocolate on top. Seal jar.

Attach the following recipe to the jar:

Chocolate Walnut Cookies

1/2 cups butter, melted
2 eggs
3 teaspoons vanilla

Remove the 3 squares of chocolate from the jar and melt in microwave. In a large bowl, combine melted chocolate, butter, eggs and vanilla. Add the contents of the jar and mix well. Roll into small balls. Bake at 350 degrees F 8 to 10 minutes.

Apricot Chews

FILLS ONE QUART GLASS JAR

1 cup dried apricots (measured after chopping)
1 tablespoon sugar
1 tablespoon flour
2 cups chopped pecans

Put the sugar and flour in the quart jar. Add pecans. Add the dried apricots on top. (Placing apricots in a small resealable plastic bag for freshness is optional.) Seal jar.

Attach the following recipe to the jar:

Apricot Chews

1 cup Eagle Brand condensed milk
2 tablespoons lemon juice

Pour the contents of the jar in a bowl. Add condensed milk and lemon juice; mix well. (The mixture will be thin and needs frequent stirring.) Drop on well-greased baking sheet in small spoonfuls. Bake at 300 degrees for 20 minutes. Remove immediately from pan. Yield: 2 dozen.

Brownie Bark Cookies

FILLS ONE PINT GLASS JAR

This recipe fits in a pint jar. The following picture shows the short pint Bell jar with a 5" square of fabric on top.

1 cup flour
1 teaspoon baking powder
1/8 teaspoon salt
1 cup sugar
2 squares unsweetened baking chocolate bar

Mix together flour, baking powder and salt in a bowl. Layer in pint jar: flour mixture, then sugar. Pack well after each layer. Lay the chocolate squares on top. Seal jar.

Attach the following recipe to the jar:

Brownie Bark Cookies

1/4 cup butter
2 eggs, beaten
1 teaspoon vanilla
Confectioners' sugar

Remove the 2 squares of chocolate from the jar. Melt butter and chocolate squares together. Pour remaining contents of jar in a bowl; mix in eggs and vanilla. Add chocolate mixture and beat well.

On a baking sheet sprayed with non-stick cooking spray, drop dough by very small (1/2") spoonfuls (dough will spread while baking). Sprinkle with confectioners' sugar. Bake at 350 degrees F for 12 minutes. Yield: Makes: 3 to 4 dozen.

Chocolate Clusters

FILLS ONE QUART GLASS JAR

1 cup peanut butter chips
1 cup chocolate chips
1 cup butterscotch chips
3/4 cup unsalted peanuts or chopped walnuts

Layer each cup of chips in a quart jar (don't pack); place nuts in a small resealable plastic bag and put bag on top of chips. Seal jar.

Attach the following recipe to the jar:

Chocolate Clusters

Remove bag of nuts from jar and set aside. Pour the remainder of the jar into a microwave-safe bowl and melt on Medium until melted. Stir occasionally. Watch carefully; don't overcook, just melt. Stir in nuts from bag. Drop candy onto waxed paper and refrigerate.

Pecan Puffs

FILLS ONE QUART GLASS JAR

1/4 cup confectioners' sugar
2 cups flour
1 cup chopped pecans

Place the ingredients in a quart jar in order listed above, packing well after the first 2 layers. Seal jar.

Attach the following recipe to the jar:

Pecan Puffs

1 cup butter, melted
2 tablespoons vanilla
1 tablespoon water
Confectioners' sugar

Pour the contents of the jar in a bowl. Add butter, vanilla, and water; mix well. Form small 1 inch balls. Bake on ungreased baking sheet at 300 degrees F for 15 to 20 minutes or until bottoms are delicately browned. While hot, roll in confectioners' sugar. Yield: 3 dozen.

M&M Cookies

FILLS ONE QUART GLASS JAR

2 cups flour
1 teaspoon salt
1 teaspoon baking soda
1/2 cup sugar
1 cup brown sugar
1 to 1 1/4 cups M&M's

Mix together flour, salt and baking soda in a bowl. Layer in quart jar: flour mixture, brown sugar and sugar. Pack well after each layer. Add the M&M's on top of sugar. Seal jar.

Attach the following recipe to the jar:

M&M Cookies

1 cup butter, melted
2 teaspoons vanilla
2 eggs

Remove the M&M's from the jar and set aside. Blend butter, vanilla and eggs; mix well. Add the remaining contents of the jar and mix well. Add 3/4 cup M&M's. Drop by spoonful on ungreased baking sheet. Slightly push a few of the remaining M&M's on each cookie before baking. Bake at 350 degrees F for 10 minutes.

Butterscotch-Oatmeal Cookie Mix

FILLS ONE QUART GLASS JAR

1 cup flour
1 teaspoon baking soda
1/8 teaspoon salt
2 cups quick cooking oats
3/4 cup white sugar
3/4 cup butterscotch chips

Mix together flour, baking soda and salt in a bowl. Layer in quart jar in this order, packing well after each layer: flour mixture, oats, sugar, then lay the chips on top (optionally the chips can be placed in a small resealable plastic bag and added to the top of the jar). Seal jar.

Attach the following recipe to the jar:

Butterscotch-Oatmeal Cookies

3/4 cup butter

Preheat oven to 350 degrees F. Carefully remove the butterscotch chips from the top of the jar. Melt the butter and butterscotch chips together in a small saucepan over low heat.
Pour contents of the jar into a bowl; add the butterscotch chip mixture. Mix until well blended. Drop by spoonful on an ungreased baking sheet. Bake 10 minutes at 350 degrees F. Cookies will be crisp.

Crisp Sugar Drop Cookies

FILLS ONE QUART GLASS JAR

2 1/2 cups flour
1/2 teaspoon baking soda
1 teaspoon salt
1 cup sugar

Combine flour, baking soda and salt. Place in quart jar. Add sugar to jar. Seal jar.

Attach the following recipe to the jar:

Crisp Sugar Drop Cookies

1 egg, beaten
2 tablespoons vinegar
1 1/2 teaspoons lemon juice
1 teaspoon vanilla
1/2 cup butter, melted

Combine egg, vinegar, lemon juice, vanilla and butter. Add contents of jar and mix well. Drop by spoonful on an ungreased baking sheet and flatten with a fork. Bake at 400 degrees F for 10 to 12 minutes.

Optional: For half chocolate-dipped cookies, melt chocolate chips in microwave. Dip the cookie in the chocolate, let drip then dry on wax paper.

Raisin-Nut Drops

FILLS ONE QUART GLASS JAR

1 (6 oz.) package semi-sweet chocolate chips
1 cup peanuts
1 cup seedless raisins

Layer each ingredient above in a quart jar. The raisins optionally can be put in a small resealable plastic bag to keep them fresh. Seal jar.

Attach the following recipe to the jar:

Raisin-Nut Drops

Place chocolate, peanuts and raisins in a 2-1/2 quart casserole dish. Cook in microwave for 1 to 3 minutes on HIGH until chocolate chips melt (watch carefully). Stir to cover peanuts and raisins completely. Drop by spoonful onto waxed paper. Place in refrigerator to set.

Butterscotch Cookies

FILLS ONE QUART GLASS JAR

1 1/8 cups all-purpose flour
1/2 teaspoon baking soda
1/4 teaspoon baking powder
1/4 teaspoon salt
1/2 cup flaked coconut
1/2 cup brown sugar, packed
1/2 cup white sugar
3/4 cup high protein crisp rice and wheat cereal (Special-K)
3/4 cup butterscotch chips
1/2 cup pecans, chopped

Mix flour, baking soda, baking powder and salt together. Put flour mixture in jar and pack. Layer coconut, brown sugar and white sugar in jar, packing each layer well. On top, place the Special-K, butterscotch chips and pecans. Seal jar.

Attach the following recipe to the jar:

Butterscotch Cookies

1/2 cup butter, softened
1 egg
1/2 teaspoon vanilla

Preheat oven to 350 degrees F. Empty cookie mix from jar into a large bowl. Add butter, egg and vanilla, and mix well. Roll into 1 1/2" balls. Place on ungreased baking sheets, then flatten each cookie ball. Bake for 8 to 10 minutes. Yield: 2 dozen.

Raisin Spice Cookies

FILLS ONE QUART GLASS JAR

1 cup all-purpose flour
1 teaspoon ground cinnamon
1 teaspoon baking soda
1/2 teaspoon ground nutmeg
1/2 teaspoon salt
3/4 cup brown sugar, packed
1/2 cup white sugar
2 cups rolled oats
1/2 cup raisins

In a bowl, mix flour, cinnamon, baking soda, nutmeg and salt. In a quart jar, layer ingredients in this order: flour mixture, brown sugar, white sugar, rolled oats. Pack firmly after each addition. Optionally, place the raisins in a small resealable plastic bag and lay on top in the jar or just add raisins on top. Seal jar.

Attach the following recipe to the jar:

Raisin Spice Cookies

3/4 cup butter or margarine, softened
1 egg, slightly beaten
1 teaspoon of vanilla

Preheat oven to 350 degrees F. Empty cookie mix from jar into a large bowl. Add butter or margarine, egg and vanilla; mix well. Shape into 1 1/2" balls. Place on a greased or parchment lined baking sheet, 2 inches apart. Bake for 11 to 13 minutes. Yield: 2 dozen.

Million Dollar Cookie Mix

FILLS ONE QUART GLASS JAR

2 cups flour
1/2 teaspoon salt
1/2 teaspoon baking soda
1/2 cup brown sugar
1/2 cup white sugar
1/2 cup chopped nuts

Mix flour, salt and baking soda together. Put flour mixture in jar and pack. Layer brown sugar, then white sugar in a quart jar, packing each layer well. On top, place the nuts. Seal jar.

Attach the following recipe to the jar:

Million Dollar Cookies

1 cup butter
1 teaspoon vanilla
1 egg
Granulated sugar

Pour contents of jar into a large bowl. Add butter, vanilla and egg. Mix and roll into small balls. Roll each ball in granulated sugar. Place on greased or parchment lined baking sheet. Flatten each with the bottom of a small glass dipped in sugar. Bake at 350 degrees F for 10 minutes.

OATMEAL

Baked Oatmeal

FILLS ONE QUART GLASS JAR

There is enough room at the top of this quart jar to add some nuts or raisins in a small resealable plastic bag if you wish.

3 cups quick cooking oats
1 tablespoon baking powder
1/2 teaspoon salt
2 tablespoons brown sugar
1/2 teaspoon cinnamon
3/4 cup white sugar

Put the oats in a quart jar and pack. In a small bowl, mix together baking powder, salt, brown sugar and cinnamon. Add to jar as the next layer. Pour white sugar on top. Seal jar.

Attach the following recipe to the jar:

Baked Oatmeal

1/2 cup applesauce or vegetable oil
2 eggs
1 cup milk

Optional – 1/2 cup chopped almonds or walnuts, coconut, diced apples, raisins, blueberries, diced peaches or a can of fruit.

Combine applesauce or oil, eggs and milk; beat well. Add the contents of the jar and stir until well mixed. Add any of the optional ingredients above. Pour into a lightly greased 8" or 9" cake pan. Sprinkle cinnamon and brown sugar on top, if desired. Refrigerate overnight.

The next morning, preheat oven to 350 degrees F. Bake for 35 minutes or until oatmeal is firm. Serve with milk.

Low Fat Oatmeal

FILLS ONE PINT GLASS JAR

This is a great all-natural recipe for those wanting to start their day in a healthy, low fat, high fiber way.

1 1/2 cups oat bran
1/4 cup + 2 tablespoons unprocessed wheat bran
3 tablespoons cinnamon

Combine oat bran, wheat bran and cinnamon; mix well. Put in pint jar and pack. Seal jar. Yield: 17 servings of oatmeal.

Attach the following recipe to the jar:

Low Fat Oatmeal

1/2 cup low fat milk
2 tablespoons mix from jar
2 tablespoons raisins or dried cranberries

Add 2 tablespoons oatmeal from the jar to 1/2 cup low fat milk and stir. Microwave, covered, for 1 minute. Add fruit and let stand 5 minutes to thicken. (optional – add 1/2 teaspoon sugar or Truvia, or 1/2 of a mashed banana) Thin with milk, as desired.

JAR MIXES

This section is all about spices and seasoning recipes to mix and give away (or keep for yourself!). In this section, the recipient does not need to do anything but cook with jar contents. Many of the seasoning mixes found at craft shows are right here.

JUST HERBS

Salad Herb Blend – No Salt

FILLS ONE HALF-PINT (8 OZ.) GLASS JAR

1/4 cup dried parsley
1/4 cup marjoram
2 1/2 tablespoons dried basil
1 1/2 tablespoons sesame seeds
1 1/2 tablespoons chili pepper flakes
1 1/2 tablespoons powdered rosemary
1 1/4 tablespoons powdered celery seed
2 1/2 teaspoons dried savory
2 1/2 teaspoons rubbed sage
2 1/4 teaspoons dried thyme
2 teaspoons onion powder
2 teaspoons dried dill weed
1 1/4 teaspoons finely ground black pepper
1/4 teaspoon garlic powder

In bowl, combine all ingredients. Pour into jar; seal jar. Makes 1 cup.

Attach the following recipe to the jar:

Salad Herb Blend – No Salt

Add herb blend to salad greens before adding dressing. Or sprinkle over pasta salad. Store jar in a cool, dry place.

**Quantity Recipe for Salad Herb Blend: *Same recipe increased to fit in 5 half pint (8 oz.) jars or 10 quarter pint jars, for your convenience:*

1 cup dried parsley
1 cup marjoram
1/2 cup + 2 tablespoons dried basil
1/4 cup + 2 tablespoons sesame seeds
1/4 cup + 2 tablespoons chili pepper flakes
1/4 cup + 2 tablespoons powdered rosemary
1/4 cup powdered celery seed
3 tablespoons + 1 teaspoon dried savory
3 tablespoons + 1 teaspoon rubbed sage
3 tablespoons dried thyme
2 tablespoons + 2 teaspoons onion powder
2 tablespoons + 2 teaspoons dried dill weed
1 tablespoon + 2 teaspoons finely ground black pepper
1 teaspoon garlic powder

By The Teaspoon Herb Seasoning

FILLS ONE QUARTER-PINT GLASS JAR

1 teaspoon cayenne pepper
6 teaspoons garlic powder
2 teaspoons dried basil
2 teaspoons dried marjoram
2 teaspoons dried thyme
2 teaspoons dried parsley
2 teaspoons dried savory
2 teaspoons mace
2 teaspoons onion powder
2 teaspoons freshly ground black pepper
2 teaspoons rubbed sage

In bowl, combine all ingredients. Pour into jar; seal jar.

Attach the following recipe to the jar:

By the Teaspoon Herb Seasoning

Use as seasoning in casseroles, stews or fresh vegetable dishes. Use 1 teaspoon or less to taste. Store jar in a cool, dry place.

**Quantity Recipe for By the Teaspoon Herb Seasoning:
Same recipe increased to fit in 4 half pint (8 oz.) jars or 8 quarter pint (4 oz.) jars, for your convenience:

2 teaspoons cayenne pepper
1/4 cup garlic powder
4 teaspoons dried basil
4 teaspoons dried marjoram
4 teaspoons dried thyme
4 teaspoons dried parsley
4 teaspoons dried savory
4 teaspoons mace
4 teaspoons onion powder
4 teaspoons freshly ground black pepper
4 teaspoons rubbed sage

All-Purpose Salt Substitute

FILLS ONE HALF-PINT (8 OZ.) GLASS JAR

This recipe makes 1 cup, which will fit in one half pint (8 oz.) jar or 2 quarter pint jars.

6 tablespoons onion powder
3 tablespoons poultry seasoning
3 tablespoons paprika
2 tablespoons dry mustard
1 tablespoon garlic powder
2 teaspoons ground oregano
2 teaspoons freshly ground black pepper
1 teaspoon chili powder

Mix all ingredients together and place in half pint jar. Seal jar.

Attach the following recipe to the jar:

All-Purpose Salt Substitute

Use this table salt alternative on all your favorite foods.

Low-Salt All-Purpose Seasoning Mix

FILLS ONE HALF-PINT (8 OZ.) GLASS JAR

This recipe makes 1 cup, which will fit in one half pint (8 oz.) jar or 2 quarter pint jars.

1 teaspoon pepper
2 teaspoons garlic powder
4 teaspoons dry mustard
4 teaspoons paprika
2 teaspoons leaf thyme, crumbled
2 teaspoons ground celery seed
8 teaspoons leaf basil, crumbled
2 teaspoons dried parsley flakes
2 teaspoons ground marjoram
2 teaspoons curry powder (optional)
3 teaspoons salt
2 tablespoons + 2 teaspoons onion powder

Mix all ingredients together and place in half pint jar. Seal jar.

Attach the following recipe to the jar:

Low-Salt All-Purpose Seasoning Mix

This delicious low salt seasoning blend is great on everything from vegetables to meats and fish. Try it on all your favorite foods.

SEASONING MIXES

Barbecue Dry Rub

FILLS ONE HALF-PINT GLASS JAR

This will fit perfectly in a half pint jar. It will be a little less than one cup of dry rub, enough for 5 or 6 times of grilling.

1/3 cup white sugar
1/3 cup brown sugar
2 tablespoons salt
1 tablespoon pepper
1 tablespoon paprika

Mix all ingredients together and place in half-pint jar. Seal jar.

Attach the following recipe to the jar:

Barbecue Dry Rub

Rub on your favorite meat before grilling. Great on country style ribs or pork chops.

Store the remaining dry rub in a cool, dry place sealed in this jar until ready to use.

Poultry Seasoning

FILLS FOUR HALF-PINT (8 OZ.) GLASS JARS

1 cup dried, crumbled sage leaves
2 cups dried parsley
1 teaspoon dried onion powder
2 tablespoons salt
1 teaspoon freshly ground pepper
1/2 cup ground rosemary
1/4 cup ground marjoram
1/2 teaspoon ground ginger

Mix all herbs and seasonings together and place in 4 half-pint jars. Seal jars.

Attach the following recipe to the jar:

Poultry Seasoning

Add 1 tablespoon of the seasoning to 1/2 cup of melted butter for rubbing over chicken or turkey before roasting, or use the same amount directly in a bread stuffing.

Cajun Spice Mix

FILLS ONE QUARTER PINT GLASS JAR

If you don't want this mix to be very spicy, leave out the red pepper flakes. Also the salt can be reduced to 1 teaspoon if your recipient is watching their salt intake.

1 tablespoon + 2 teaspoons paprika
1 tablespoon + 1 teaspoon garlic powder
1 tablespoon salt
2 teaspoons onion powder
2 teaspoons cayenne pepper
2 teaspoons ground black pepper
2 1/2 teaspoons dried thyme
2 1/2 teaspoons dried oregano
1 teaspoon red pepper flakes (optional)

Mix all herbs and seasonings together and place a quarter pint jar. Seal jar.

Attach the following recipe to the jar:

Cajun Spice

Use this Cajun spice mix to season chicken, seafood, steaks or vegetables. Great for Cajun shrimp or mix with mayonnaise for Cajun spiced burgers. Spice up red beans and rice or sprinkle on tater tots or potatoes. Also a great spice for chicken wings and jambalaya. Keep on hand for summer barbeques as a rub for meats and fish. Even popcorn perks up with this lively spice.

**Quantity Recipe for Cajun Spice Mix: *Same recipe increased to fit in 4 half pint (8 oz.) jars or 8 quarter pint jars, for your convenience:*

3/4 cup + 1 tablespoon + 1 teaspoon paprika
2/3 cup garlic powder
1/2 cup salt
1/3 cup onion powder
1/3 cup cayenne pepper
1/3 cup ground black pepper
1/3 cup + 1 tablespoon + 1 teaspoon dried thyme
1/3 cup + 1 tablespoon + 1 teaspoon dried oregano
2 tablespoons + 2 teaspoons red pepper flakes (optional)

Shake-It-And-Bake-It Mix

FILLS 5 HALF-PINT (8 OZ.) GLASS JARS

2 cups flour
2 cups cornmeal
3 tablespoons ground cumin
4 teaspoons onion powder
4 teaspoons garlic powder
4 teaspoons dried oregano, crushed
2 teaspoons cayenne pepper
2 teaspoons salt
2 teaspoons freshly ground black pepper

Mix all ingredients together and place in 5 half pint jars. Seal jars.

Attach the following recipe to the jar:

Shake-It-And-Bake-It

To season a 3-pound chicken, place 1/2 cup of the mix in a large plastic bag. Cut the chicken into serving pieces and place a few pieces into the bag at a time, shaking to coat. Bake for about one hour at 375 degrees F, turning several times.

Taco Seasoning Mix

FILLS ONE HALF-PINT (8 OZ.) GLASS JAR

1/4 cup instant minced onion
2 tablespoons salt
2 tablespoons + 2 teaspoons chili powder
1 tablespoon + 1 teaspoon cornstarch
1 tablespoon + 1 teaspoon crushed dried red pepper flakes
1 tablespoon + 1 teaspoon instant minced garlic
2 teaspoons dried oregano
1 tablespoon + 1 teaspoon ground cumin

Mix all ingredients together and place in half-pint jar. Seal jar.

Attach the following recipe to the jar:

Taco Filling

1 lb. lean ground beef
1/2 cup water
2 tablespoons taco seasoning mix from jar

Brown ground beef in a skillet over medium-high heat. Drain grease. Add water and taco seasoning mix. Simmer on medium for 10 minutes, stirring occasionally. Yield: 8 tacos. Can also be used for enchiladas, shredded chicken or meatloaf.

Spaghetti Seasoning Mix

FILLS ONE HALF-PINT (8 OZ.) GLASS JAR

1/4 cup parsley flakes
1/4 cup instant minced onion
1/4 cup cornstarch
2 tablespoons + 2 teaspoons green pepper flakes
2 tablespoons salt
1 tablespoon + 1 teaspoon sugar
1 teaspoon instant minced garlic
1 tablespoon Italian seasoning or combination of Italian herbs (oregano, thyme, sage, basil, marjoram, rosemary)

Mix all ingredients together and place in half pint jar. Seal jar.

Attach the following recipe to the jar:

Spaghetti Sauce

1 lb. lean ground beef
3 cups tomato juice or water
2 (8-oz.) cans tomato sauce
1 (6-oz.) can tomato paste
1/3 cup spaghetti seasoning mix from jar

Brown ground beef in a skillet over medium-high heat. Drain grease. Mix in tomato juice or water, tomato sauce and tomato paste. Stir in 1/3 cup spaghetti seasoning mix from jar. Reduce heat and simmer 30 minutes, stirring occasionally. Yield: 4 to 6 servings. Spaghetti seasoning mix can also be used in lasagna and pizza sauce.

Sloppy Joe Seasoning

FILLS ONE HALF-PINT (8 OZ.) GLASS JAR

1/4 cup + 3 tablespoons instant minced onion
2 tablespoons + 1 teaspoon green pepper flakes
2 tablespoons + 1 teaspoon cornstarch
2 tablespoons + 1 teaspoon salt
1 tablespoon + 1/2 teaspoon instant minced garlic
1 3/4 teaspoons celery seed
1 3/4 teaspoons dry mustard
1 3/4 teaspoons chili powder

Mix all ingredients together and place in half-pint jar. Seal jar.

Attach the following recipe to the jar:

Sloppy Joes

1 lb. lean ground beef
3 tablespoons sloppy joe seasoning mix from jar
1 (8-oz.) can tomato sauce
1/2 cup water
6 hamburger buns

Brown ground beef in a skillet over medium-high heat and drain grease. Add seasoning mix, water and tomato sauce. Bring to a boil. Reduce heat to medium-low and simmer about 10 minutes, stirring occasionally. Serve on hamburger buns. Yield: 6 servings.

Fajita Seasoning

FILLS ONE HALF-PINT (8 OZ.) GLASS JAR

1/4 cup and 1 tablespoon cornstarch
3 tablespoons and 1 teaspoon chili powder
1 tablespoon and 2 teaspoons paprika
1 tablespoon and 2 teaspoons salt
1 tablespoon and 2 teaspoons white sugar
2-1/2 teaspoons ground cumin
2-1/2 teaspoons garlic powder
2-1/2 teaspoons onion powder
1 teaspoon cayenne pepper

Mix all ingredients together and place in half-pint jar. Seal jar.

Attach the following recipe to the jar:

Fajitas

1/4 cup water
4 tablespoons fajita seasoning from jar

Mix water and fajita seasoning together and sprinkle over beef or chicken strips while cooking. Add onions and peppers.

Herbed Cream Cheese Spread

FILLS ONE QUARTER-PINT GLASS JAR

4 teaspoons dried chives
4 teaspoons caraway seed
4 teaspoons dried dill
4 teaspoons dried basil
2 teaspoons garlic powder
1/2 teaspoon black pepper

Mix all ingredients together and place in quarter pint jar. Seal jar.

Attach the following recipe to the jar:

Herbed Cream Cheese Spread

1 (8 oz.) package cream cheese, softened
4 1/2 teaspoons of herb mix from jar

Blend herb mix from jar into softened cream cheese. Form into a ball. Keep refrigerated. Serve with assorted crackers or pretzel sticks. This jar mix will make 4 cheese balls.

Farmhouse Buttermilk Dressing

FILLS ONE HALF-PINT (8 OZ.) GLASS JAR

1/4 cup + 1 1/2 tablespoons dried parsley
3 tablespoons salt
1 tablespoon + 1 1/2 teaspoons dried chives
1 tablespoon + 1 1/2 teaspoons dried oregano
1 tablespoon + 1 1/2 teaspoons dried tarragon
1 tablespoon + 1 1/2 teaspoons garlic powder
1 tablespoon + 1 1/2 teaspoons pepper
1 tablespoon + 1 1/2 teaspoons dried cilantro

Mix all ingredients together and place in half pint jar. Seal jar.

Attach the following recipe to the jar:

Farmhouse Buttermilk Dressing Mix

1/2 cup mayonnaise
1/2 cup buttermilk
1 tablespoon Buttermilk Dressing Mix from jar

Blend mayonnaise and buttermilk; stir in dressing mix. Refrigerate until ready to use.

Dry Italian Seasoning Mix

FILLS ONE HALF-PINT GLASS JAR

4 tablespoons dried oregano
3 tablespoons salt
2 tablespoons garlic powder
2 tablespoons dried parsley
2 tablespoons white sugar
2 tablespoons onion powder
2 teaspoons dried basil
2 teaspoons ground black pepper
1 teaspoon black pepper
1/2 teaspoon celery salt
1/2 teaspoon dried thyme

Combine all ingredients and place in half pint jar. Seal jar. Yield: 1 cup.

Attach the following recipe to the jar:

Use jar mix as is in any recipe that calls for Italian seasoning.

Italian Dressing

1/4 cup white vinegar
1/2 to 2/3 cup olive oil or canola oil
2 tablespoons water

Combine vinegar, oil and water in a container with a lid. Add 2 tablespoons of Italian seasoning mix from jar and shake well. This is also good as a bread dip.

Thousand Island or Ranch Dressing

FILLS 4 HALF-PINT GLASS JARS

1 1/4 cups dried parsley flakes
5/8 cup onion powder
5/8 cup saltine crackers, finely crushed
5/8 cup garlic powder
5/8 cup dried minced onion
1/3 cup onion salt
1/3 cup garlic salt
2 1/2 tablespoons dill weed

Mix all ingredients together and place in jars. Seal jar.

Attach the following recipe to the jar:

Thousand Island or Ranch Dressing

***To make Ranch Dressing*:**
2 cups buttermilk
2 cups mayonnaise
2 tablespoons of mix from jar

Combine all ingredients. Keep refrigerated. Yield: 4 cups.

***To make Thousand Island Dressing*:**
2 cups buttermilk
2 cups mayonnaise

1 cup chili sauce
1/2 cup sweet pickle relish
2 tablespoons of mix from jar

Combine all ingredients. Keep refrigerated. Yield: 5 1/2 cups.

Chili Seasoning Mix

FILLS ONE QUARTER-PINT GLASS JAR

If your recipient doesn't like it hot, decrease the red pepper in the recipe below to 1 teaspoon.

2 tablespoons chili powder
1 tablespoon crushed red pepper
1 tablespoon + 1 teaspoon dried minced onion
1 tablespoon + 1 teaspoon dried minced garlic
3 teaspoons white sugar
3 teaspoons ground cumin
3 teaspoons dried parsley
3 teaspoons salt
1 1/4 teaspoons dried basil
1/4 teaspoon ground black pepper

Mix all ingredients together and place in quarter pint jar. Seal jar.

Attach the following recipe to the jar:

Chili

1 lb. hamburger
2 tablespoons of chili seasoning from jar
1 (14.5 oz.) can diced tomatoes
1 (15 oz.) can tomato sauce
1 can Ranch style beans, drained and rinsed

In a large saucepan, brown hamburger; drain grease. Add 2 tablespoons of seasoning from the jar, tomatoes and tomato sauce and simmer on low for 1/2 hour or longer. Add beans and simmer for 15 to 30 minutes longer. Can also be made in a slow cooker.

Chicken or Beef Gravy Mix

FILLS TWO HALF-PINT GLASS JARS

1 (2 1/4 oz.) jar instant chicken or beef bouillon granules
1 1/2 cups all-purpose flour
3/4 teaspoon pepper
2 teaspoons onion powder
2 teaspoons garlic powder

Combine bouillon, flour and pepper. Place in half pint jar. Seal jar.

Attach the following recipe to the jar:

To Make Gravy:

1 1/2 cups water
3 tablespoons margarine or butter

In a saucepan, melt butter or margarine, then add 1/4 cup of gravy mix from jar. Cook and stir until lightly browned, about 1 minute. Whisk in water until smooth. Bring to a boil; cook and stir until thickened, about 2 minutes. Yield: 1 1/2 cups.

Brown Gravy Mix

FILLS TWO HALF-PINT GLASS JARS

5 tablespoons beef bouillon granules
1 3/8 cups cornstarch
1 1/3 teaspoons instant coffee crystals
1 1/2 teaspoons onion powder
1 teaspoon garlic powder
1/2 teaspoon paprika
1/2 teaspoon black pepper

Combine all ingredients; mix well. Place in two half-pint jars. Seal jar.

Attach the following recipe to the jar:

To Make Gravy:

1 1/2 cups water
3 tablespoons brown gravy mix from jar

In a saucepan, add water plus 3 tablespoons gravy mix from jar. Bring to a boil; cook and stir until thickened, about 1 minute.

Cajun Fry Mix

FILLS ONE PINT GLASS JAR

1 cup flour
2/3 cup corn flour
1/3 cup corn meal
1 tablespoon + 1 teaspoon Old Bay seasoning
1 tablespoon baking powder
1 tablespoon salt
1 tablespoon onion powder
1 tablespoon garlic powder
1/2 teaspoon cayenne pepper

Mix all ingredients together and place in pint jar. Seal jar.

Attach the following recipe to the jar:

Cajun Fry

Toss your favorite veggies, fish, shellfish, or even cheese in this seasoned mixture to coat before frying. For thicker breading, dip in a mixture of 1 cup milk and 1 beaten egg before rolling in Cajun Fry mix.

BREAD DIPPING MIXES

Italian Bread Dipping Blend

FILLS ONE HALF-PINT GLASS JAR

2 tablespoons black pepper
2 tablespoons dried oregano
2 tablespoons dried rosemary
2 tablespoons dried basil
2 tablespoons dried parsley
2 tablespoons garlic powder
2 tablespoons minced garlic
2 tablespoons crushed red pepper (optional)
2 teaspoons salt

Mix all ingredients together. Using a mortar & pestle, coffee grinder or food processor, grind the mixture until all ingredients are about the same consistency. Place in half pint jar. Seal jar.

Attach the following recipe to the jar:

Italian Bread Dipping Blend

To use, put 1 tablespoon of bread dipping blend on a small plate. Pour 5 to 6 tablespoons extra virgin olive oil over it and blend together. Add fresh Italian bread. Also try adding a little melted butter to the olive oil.

Tuscan Bread Dipping Mix

FILLS ONE HALF-PINT GLASS JAR

1/4 cup finely minced garlic
1/4 cup dried rosemary
1/4 cup dried thyme
1/4 cup dried basil
1 teaspoon pepper
1 teaspoon salt

Mix all ingredients together. Using a mortar & pestle, coffee grinder or food processor, grind the mixture until all ingredients are about the same consistency. Place in half pint jar. Seal jar.

Attach the following recipe to the jar:

Tuscan Bread Dipping Blend

1/4 cup olive oil
1/2 teaspoon sun-dried tomato paste
1 teaspoon mix from jar

In a bowl, pour the olive oil and add 1 teaspoon of Tuscan bread dipping mix from the jar to the oil mixture. Stir the spices into the oil. Add tomato paste in the center of bowl.

DIP MIXES

These recipes that will fit in one half pint (8 oz.) jar can also be halved and placed in 2 quarter pint jars.

Bacon-Flavored Dip Mix

FILLS ONE HALF-PINT GLASS JAR

1/2 cup instant bacon bits
1/4 cup instant minced onion
1 tablespoon + 1 teaspoon instant beef bouillon
1/2 teaspoon instant minced garlic

Mix all ingredients together and place in half pint jar. Seal jar.

Attach the following recipe to the jar:

Bacon-Flavored Dip

Vary this dip by substituting sour cream with an 8-oz. package softened cream cheese or 1 cup of plain yogurt.

1 cup sour cream
3 tablespoons dip mix from jar

Combine sour cream and bacon-flavored dip mix. Refrigerate for 1/2 hour before serving. Yield: 1 cup.

Onion Dip Mix

FILLS ONE HALF-PINT GLASS JAR

1/4 cup + 1 tablespoon instant minced onion
1/2 cup instant beef bouillon
1 teaspoon +1/4 teaspoon garlic salt

Mix all ingredients together and place in a half pint jar. Seal jar.

Attach the following recipe to the jar:

Onion Dip

1 cup sour cream or 8 oz. package of cream cheese, softened
1 tablespoon grated Parmesan cheese
3 tablespoons onion dip mix from jar

Combine sour cream or cream cheese, Parmesan cheese and onion dip mix from jar. Refrigerate for 1/2 hour before serving. Yield: 1 cup.

Ranch-Style Seasoning

FILLS ONE QUARTER-PINT GLASS JAR

2 tablespoons + 2 teaspoons dried parsley
4 teaspoons ground black pepper
4 teaspoons garlic powder
2 teaspoons seasoned salt
2 teaspoons sea salt
2 teaspoons onion powder
1 teaspoon dried thyme
1 teaspoon dill weed

Mix all ingredients together and place in a quarter pint jar. Seal jar.

Attach the following recipe to the jar:

Ranch-Style Seasoning

FOR RANCH DIP: Mix one tablespoon seasoning from jar with 1 3/4 cups sour cream and 1/4 cup of buttermilk.

-OR-

FOR RANCH DIP: Mix one tablespoon seasoning from jar with 1/4 cup buttermilk, 1 8 oz. container fat-free plain yogurt and 1/2 cup light mayonnaise.

FOR RANCH DRESSING: Mix one tablespoon seasoning from jar with 1 cup mayonnaise and 1 cup buttermilk.

Use one tablespoon of seasoning in place of one package of Ranch dressing mix in recipes.

**Quantity Recipe for Ranch-Style Seasoning: *Same recipe increased to fit in 6 quarter-pint jars, for your convenience:*

1 cup dried parsley
1/2 cup ground black pepper
1/2 cup garlic powder
1/4 cup seasoned salt
1/4 cup sea salt
1/4 cup onion powder
2 tablespoons dried thyme
2 tablespoons dill weed

Southwest Fiesta Dip Mix

FILLS ONE PINT GLASS JAR

1/2 cup dried parsley
1/3 cup chili powder
1/3 cup minced onion
1/4 cup salt
1/4 cup ground cumin
1/4 cup dried chives

Mix all ingredients together and place in pint jar. Seal jar.

Attach the following recipe to the jar:

Southwest Fiesta Dip

1 cup sour cream or plain yogurt
1 cup mayonnaise
3 tablespoons fiesta dip mix from jar

Combine dip mix from jar with sour cream or yogurt and mayonnaise. Whisk until smooth. Refrigerate for a few hours before serving. Serve with fresh vegetables, tortilla chips, taquitos, fish tacos, onion rings or fried pickles. Yield: 2 cups.

Southwest Fiesta Dip

1 cup sour cream or plain yogurt
1 cup mayonnaise

Combine 3 tablespoons of
Mexican Fiesta Dip from jar with
sour cream or yogurt and
mayonnaise. Whisk until smooth.
Refrigerate for a few hours before
serving. Serve with fresh
vegetables or tortilla chips.

Vegetable Dip Mix

FILLS ONE HALF-PINT GLASS JAR

1/2 cup dried chives
1 tablespoon + 1 teaspoon dill weed
2 tablespoons + 2 teaspoons garlic salt
1 tablespoon + 1 teaspoon paprika

Mix all ingredients together and place in half pint jar. Seal jar.

Attach the following recipe to the jar:

Vegetable Dip

1 tablespoon lemon juice
1 cup mayonnaise
1 cup sour cream
2 tablespoons vegetable dip mix from jar

Combine all ingredients. Refrigerate for 1/2 hour before serving. Yield: 2 cups.

Smoked Salmon Spread

FILLS 4 HALF-PINT GLASS JARS

2 (8 oz.) packages cream cheese, softened
1 teaspoon Worcestershire sauce
1 teaspoon dill weed
3 tablespoons chopped green onion
3 drops hot pepper sauce
12 ounces smoked salmon, chopped

In a medium bowl, combine cream cheese, Worcestershire sauce, dill weed, onion and pepper sauce. Add salmon; mix well. Put into jars, cover and store in refrigerator.

JAR FILLS

This section is food items to make and fill the jars with. The recipient only has to open and eat!

JAMS AND SAUCES

The following jams and sauces are not ones that need boiled water bath canning or sterilizing. These are merely foods that can be packed in jars and will last in the refrigerator for a few weeks. The labels include the words "Refrigerate" so your recipient knows they need to be kept cool.

A little about expiration dates:

Your jam should last for 3 weeks in the refrigerator. Also look at the best-before or best-by date of the ingredients you are using to make the jam or sauce, and this will give you a clue on how long your jam will last. You may want to write an expiration date on the label of the jam.

Once a liquid begins to form on the top of the jam, your jam will go downhill quickly. The consistency will become thicker and color become darker. It can then develop an unpleasant odor, flavor then mold. At that point, the entire jar must be disposed of.

Pumpkin Butter

FILLS 5 HALF-PINT GLASS JARS

1 (29 oz.) can pumpkin puree
1 1/2 cups white sugar
3/4 cup apple juice
2 teaspoons ground cinnamon
2 teaspoons ground ginger
1 teaspoon ground nutmeg
1/2 teaspoon ground cloves

In a large saucepan, combine all ingredients; mix well. Bring mixture to a boil. Reduce heat; simmer for 30 minutes or until thickened, stirring frequently. Pour into half pint jars. Refrigerate.

Add pumpkin butter to yogurt, make a pumpkin and peanut butter sandwich, spread it on waffles, mix it with cream cheese as a spread for bread or graham crackers, even try it with cream in your coffee! Keep refrigerated.

Banana Jam

FILLS ONE PINT GLASS JAR

3 cups sliced, ripe bananas
1 1/2 cups sugar
1/4 cup orange juice
3 tablespoons lemon juice
1/4 teaspoon ground nutmeg
1/4 teaspoon cinnamon
2 whole cloves

Combine all ingredients in a deep bowl. Microwave on HIGH until sugar dissolves, 5 to 10 minutes, stirring several times. Continue cooking on HIGH until thickened, about 8 to 12 minutes. Pour into jars and let stand until set. Refrigerate. Yield: 1 pint.

Pineapple Jam

FILLS 2 PINT AND 1 HALF-PINT GLASS JARS

1 (20-ounce) can unsweetened, crushed pineapple
3 1/4 cups sugar
1/2 lemon, thinly sliced
3 ounces liquid fruit pectin
1 cup chopped walnuts (optional)

Combine ingredients except nuts and microwave on HIGH for 12 to 15 minutes or until pineapple is no longer crisp. Add walnuts and stir until thickened. Pour into jars, cover and store in refrigerator. Yield: 5 cups.

Caramel Sauce

FILLS 2 HALF-PINT GLASS JARS

Delicious with ice cream, apples and cinnamon rolls. Warm before serving. Keep refrigerated.

1/3 cup water
1 1/2 cups white sugar
2 tablespoons unsalted butter
1 1/4 cups heavy cream
1/2 teaspoon vanilla extract
1/8 teaspoon salt

In a large saucepan, simmer water, sugar and butter over medium heat. Don't stir the mixture until the sugar is completely dissolved in the water. Cook uncovered for 5 to 10 minutes, stirring occasionally, until the mixture is golden brown.

Stirring constantly, carefully and gradually pour the cream into the mixture. The hot mixture will quickly boil when the cream is added and solidify in spots. Add the vanilla extract and salt. Continue stirring over low heat for 5 to 10 minutes until the mixture is creamy and smooth. Pour into jars and cool for 1/2 hour. Refrigerate.

Hot Fudge Sauce

FILLS 2 HALF-PINT GLASS JARS

1/2 cup cocoa
3/4 cup sugar
2/3 cup milk or water
1/3 cup light corn syrup
1/3 cup butter or margarine
1 teaspoon vanilla

In a medium saucepan, mix cocoa and sugar together. Add milk or water and corn syrup; mix well. Cook over medium heat until mixture boils, stirring constantly. Boil and stir for one minute. Remove pan from heat and mix in butter or margarine and vanilla. Pour into jars, cover and store in refrigerator. Yield: 2 cups.

Apple Dip

FILLS 3 HALF-PINT GLASS JARS

1 cup brown sugar
2 (8 oz.) packages cream cheese, softened
2 tablespoons vanilla extract

Mix together the brown sugar, cream cheese and vanilla extract until the sugar has dissolved and the apple dip is smooth. Put in jars, cover and store in refrigerator. Yield: 3 cups.

SOUP

Special Cream Soup Mix

FILLS ONE QUART GLASS JAR

2 cups dry powdered milk
3/4 cup cornstarch
1/4 cup instant chicken bouillon granules (can use low sodium or no sodium)
2 tablespoons onion flakes
1 teaspoon thyme
1 teaspoon basil
1/4 teaspoon Mrs. Dash seasoning or 1/4 teaspoon white pepper

Mix all ingredients together and place in quart jar. Seal jar.

Attach the following recipe to the jar:

Special Cream Soup

For soup, mix 1/3 cup mix from jar with 1 1/2 cups cold water. Heat over low heat until mixture thickens.

For different flavor soup, add to the above one of the following:

Celery soup – 1/3 cup minced celery
Mushroom soup – 1/4 cup minced or sliced mushrooms

Potato soup – 1 cup diced and cooked potatoes
Chicken soup – 1/4 cup minced cooked chicken
Vegetable soup – 3/4 cup cooked vegetables

Cook over low heat, stirring frequently, until ingredients are tender and soup is hot.

Chicken Tortilla Soup Mix

FILLS ONE QUART GLASS JAR

1 cup white or brown long grain rice
3 cups tortilla chips, slightly crushed
1/4 cup dried chopped or minced onion
2 tablespoons chicken bouillon granules
1 teaspoon sugar
1 teaspoon chili powder
1 teaspoon dried cilantro leaves
1 teaspoon lemon pepper
1/2 teaspoon salt
1/2 teaspoon pepper
1/2 teaspoon garlic powder
1/2 teaspoon ground cumin

Add rice to a quart jar. Place the crushed tortilla chips in a small resealable plastic bag. In a small bowl, mix the onion, chicken bouillon, sugar, chili powder, cilantro, lemon pepper, salt, pepper, garlic powder and cumin; place the seasonings in another small resealable plastic bag. Add the 2 plastic bags to the quart jar. Seal jar.

Attach the following recipe to the jar:

Chicken Tortilla Soup

10 cups water
1 (14 1/2 oz.) can Mexican-style stewed tomatoes
1 (4 oz.) can diced green chilies
1 (5 oz.) can chicken, drained
Optional - 1 (15 oz.) can black beans, rinsed and drained

Remove tortilla chips from the jar; set aside. Combine water, tomatoes, rice from jar and seasoning packet from the jar in a Dutch oven or large saucepan. Bring to a boil over high heat; reduce heat, cover and simmer for 20 minutes or until rice is tender.

Add can of chicken to the pot (and optional beans) and heat thoroughly. Sprinkle crushed tortilla chips over each serving. Yield: 3 quarts.

Chicken Noodle Soup

FILLS ONE PINT GLASS JAR

1 cup fine egg noodles, uncooked
1 1/2 tablespoons chicken bouillon
1/2 teaspoon black pepper
1/4 teaspoon thyme
1/8 teaspoon garlic powder
1/8 teaspoon celery seeds
1 bay leaf

Mix all the spices together with the bouillon and place in a pint jar. Add egg noodles on top. Seal jar.

Attach the following recipe to the jar:

Chicken Noodle Soup

8 cups water
2 stalks celery, diced
2 carrots, diced
1/4 cup minced onion
3 cups cooked, diced chicken

Combine contents of jar and water in a large Dutch oven. Add celery, carrots and onion; bring to a boil. Cover the soup and simmer for 15 minutes. Discard bay leaf. Stir in the chicken and simmer an additional 5 minutes.

Good Will Soup Mix

FILLS ONE QUART GLASS JAR

1/2 cup dry split peas
1/3 cup beef bouillon granules
2 teaspoons Italian seasoning
1/4 cup pearl barley
1/2 cup dry lentils
1/4 cup dried minced onion
1/2 cup uncooked long-grain rice
1/2 cup alphabet macaroni, or other small macaroni

Mix beef bouillon with Italian seasoning. Put split peas in a quart jar, followed by the beef bouillon mixture. Then add to jar in this order: barley, lentils, onion, rice and macaroni. (The macaroni can be placed in a small resealable plastic bag for convenience of removal.) Seal jar.

Attach the following recipe to the jar:

Good Will Soup

1 lb. ground beef
1 (28 oz.) can diced tomatoes, undrained
3 quarts water (12 cups)

Remove macaroni from top of jar; set aside. Brown beef In a Dutch oven; drain. Add tomatoes, water and remaining contents of jar. Bring to a boil. Cover and reduce heat. Simmer for 45 minutes, stirring occasionally. Add macaroni and continue cooking, covered, for 15 minutes or until macaroni, peas and beans are tender.

Country Bean Soup Mix

FILLS ONE QUART GLASS JAR

Be sure to pick through the beans before adding them to the jar, making sure there are no stones or non-bean items mixed in. Just spread out each 1/2 cup of beans on a baking sheet before adding them to the jar to sort through them.

1/2 cup black-eyed peas
1/2 cup small red beans
1/2 cup black beans
1/2 cup white beans
1/2 cup split peas
1/2 cup pinto beans
1/2 cup lentils
1/4 cup dried parsley flakes
1/4 cup dried minced onion
1 teaspoon dried basil
1 teaspoon garlic powder
3 beef bouillon cubes
2 bay leaves

In a quart jar, layer beans in separate layers or mix beans together and add to jar. Mix the parsley flakes, onion, basil and garlic powder together; place in a small resealable plastic bag. Add the bouillon cubes (unwrapped) and bay leaves to the plastic bag. Put the bag in the jar; seal jar.

Attach the following recipe to the jar:

Country Bean Soup

8 cups water
1 (14 oz.) can chopped tomatoes, undrained
Salt and pepper

Remove the spice packet from jar; set aside. Place the remaining contents of the jar in a Dutch oven and add water. Be sure beans are covered with water and about 1" over. Bring to a rapid boil and boil for 2 minutes. Remove from heat, cover and let the beans sit, covered for one hour. Drain and rinse the beans.

Add the 8 cups of water, contents of spice packet from jar and chopped tomatoes in juice. Bring to a boil over high heat, then reduce heat and simmer about 2 to 2 1/2 hours until beans are tender. Remove bay leaves and season with salt and pepper.

Onion Soup Mix

FILLS ONE HALF-PINT GLASS JAR

3/4 cup dried minced onion
1/3 cup beef bouillon granules
1/4 teaspoon celery salt
1/4 teaspoon sugar
4 teaspoons onion powder

Mix all ingredients together and place in a half-pint jar. Pack and seal jar.

Attach the following recipe to the jar:

Onion Soup:

To Make Onion Soup:

Combine 4 cups water with 5 tablespoons soup mix from the jar. Bring to a boil; simmer, uncovered, for 10 minutes.

To Make Roasted Potatoes:

Toss 5 tablespoons soup mix from the jar with peeled and cubed potatoes and 1/3 cup olive oil. Spoon onto a 10x15-inch baking sheet. Bake at 450 degrees for 35 to 40 minutes, or until potatoes are tender.

To Make Onion Dip:

Blend 5 tablespoons soup mix from the jar with 2 cups sour cream. Stir well and refrigerate at least 2 hours. Stir again before serving with fresh vegetables or potato chips.

RICE AND STUFFING

Herbed Rice Mix

FILLS ONE PINT GLASS JAR

1 1/3 cups long-grain rice
1/4 cup + 2 tablespoons dried celery flakes
2 tablespoons dried minced onion
1 tablespoon + 2 teaspoons dried parsley flakes
1 teaspoon dried chives
1/2 teaspoon dried tarragon
3/4 teaspoon salt
1/2 teaspoon pepper

Mix all ingredients together and place in pint jar. Seal jar.

Attach the following recipe to the jar:

Herbed Rice

2/3 cups water
1 teaspoon butter or margarine

To prepare 1 serving of rice:
In a saucepan over medium heat, bring water and butter to a boil. Add 1/4 cup rice mixture from jar. Reduce heat; cover and simmer for 20 minutes. Remove from heat and let stand for about 5 minutes, or until liquid is absorbed. Yield: 8 servings.

Wild and Crazy Rice Mix

FILLS 5 PINT GLASS JARS

3 cups wild rice
2 cups golden raisins
1 cup brown rice
1 cup dry lentils
2 cups barley, quick-cooking
3 tablespoons dried parsley flakes
1/4 teaspoon pepper
3 tablespoons instant beef bouillon granules
2 tablespoons dried minced onion
1 tablespoon dried sweet basil
2 teaspoons dried minced garlic
1/2 teaspoon ground allspice

Rinse wild rice, brown rice and lentils and place in a large baking pan. Dry in a 300 degree F oven for about 15 minutes. Stir for even drying. When completely dry, remove from oven and cool. Combine rice and lentils with remaining ingredients. Put in 5 pint glass jars. Seal jars.

Attach the following recipe to the jar:

Wild and Crazy Rice

3 cups water
1 cup sliced mushrooms
1 cup sliced carrots
1/2 cup pecans, toasted & chopped

Combine 1 cup of rice mix from jar with water in a saucepan. Bring to a boil. Cover and reduce heat; simmer 30 minutes.

Add mushrooms, carrots and pecans. Simmer 20 to 30 minutes, or until tender. Yield: 6 servings.

Jambalaya Mix
FILLS ONE PINT GLASS JAR

1 1/4 cups raw long-grain rice
1 tablespoon parsley
1 tablespoon dried bell pepper flakes
1 bay leaf
2 tablespoons instant minced onion
1 tablespoon Cajun seasoning
2 1/2 teaspoons chicken bouillon granules
1 teaspoon salt
1/2 teaspoon ground black pepper
1/2 teaspoon garlic powder
1/2 teaspoon red pepper flakes

Combine all ingredients except rice and bay leaf. Put rice in a pint jar; add the combined spices on top of rice. Lay bay leaf on top. Seal jar.

Attach the following recipe to the jar:

Jambalaya

3 cups water
1 (16 oz.) can crushed Italian tomatoes
10 oz. Andouille sausage, sliced
1/2 cup cooked shrimp

In a large saucepan, bring the water to a boil. Add contents of jar and Italian tomatoes to saucepan. Reduce heat to simmer; add sausage and cook for 20 minutes or until rice is tender. Add shrimp and cook 5 minutes more. Remove and discard bay leaf. Yield: 8 cups.

Instant Stuffing Mix

FILLS ONE QUART GLASS JAR

3 1/2 cups unseasoned, toasted bread cubes
3 tablespoons dried celery flakes
1 tablespoon dried parsley
2 teaspoons chicken bouillon granules
2 teaspoons dried minced onion
1/4 teaspoon rubbed sage
1/4 teaspoon poultry seasoning

Place bread cubes in a quart jar. In a small bowl, combine celery flakes, parsley, bouillon, minced onion, sage and poultry seasoning; mix well. Put the seasonings in a small resealable plastic bag. Add seasonings bag on top of bread cubes. Seal jar.

Attach the following recipe to the jar:

Instant Stuffing

1 cup water
2 tablespoons butter or margarine

In a saucepan, bring water, butter or margarine and contents of seasoning packet from the jar to a boil. Reduce heat; cover and simmer for 10 minutes. Remove from heat; add bread cubes from the jar and mix gently. Cover and let stand 5 minutes. Toss with a fork before serving. Yield: 6 servings.

Pizza Crust

FILLS ONE QUART GLASS JAR

2 3/4 cups bread flour
1 package active dry yeast (1 tablespoon)
2 teaspoons salt

Mix all ingredients together and place in a quart jar. Seal jar.

Attach the following recipe to the jar:

Pizza Crust

(Makes 2 (12") pizzas)

2 tablespoons olive oil
1 cup warm water
1 cup tomato sauce
1/2 cup grated Mozzarella cheese
1/3 cup grated Parmesan cheese
1 teaspoon oregano

Place the pizza dough mix from the jar in a large bowl; add oil and water. Beat with a spoon until the mixture shapes into a ball. Knead on a floured surface for 5 minutes. Transfer to a greased bowl and let the dough rise for 90 minutes for thin crust; 2 hours to 2 hours 15 minutes for thicker crust. Divide the dough in half and pat into 2 12-inch circles. Place on baking sheets or pizza baking pans.

Top the pizza dough with tomato sauce, oregano and cheeses. Bake at 425 degrees in a preheated oven for 20 to 25 minutes. Let stand 5 minutes before cutting.

Pancake Mix

FILLS ONE PINT GLASS JAR

2 cups all-purpose flour
4 tablespoons sugar
5 teaspoons baking powder
1 teaspoon salt

Combine all ingredients and place in a pint jar. Seal jar.

Attach the following recipe to the jar:

Pancake Mix

2 eggs
1/2 cup oil
2 cups milk

In a large bowl, pour the pancake mix from jar; add eggs, oil and milk. Stir until well mixed.

Spray a large skillet or griddle with non-stick cooking spray. Heat griddle over medium heat. Pour 1/4 cup batter onto the griddle. Cook until bubbles form on the surface, then turn over with a spatula and cook to a golden brown color.

These pancakes freeze well after they are cooked. Place each pancake separately in a small resealable plastic bag and place all the small bags in a large freezer-safe resealable plastic bag. Reheat in microwave oven.

DRINKS

Bavarian Mint Coffee

FILLS ONE HALF-PINT GLASS JAR

1/3 cup granulated sugar
1/4 cup instant nonfat powdered dry milk
1/4 cup instant coffee
2 tablespoons unsweetened cocoa powder
2 hard peppermint candies, crushed

Mix all ingredients together. In a blender or a food processor, grind the mixture until all ingredients are about the same consistency. Place in a half-pint jar. Seal jar.

Attach the following recipe to the jar:

Bavarian Mint Coffee
In a cup, combine 2 tablespoons of the Bavarian Mint Coffee mix with 2/3 cup of boiling water.

Vanilla Hot Chocolate

FILLS ONE HALF-PINT GLASS JAR

2 teaspoons pure vanilla powder
2 teaspoons dried orange peel
1 cup white chocolate chips

In a small bowl, combine all ingredients. Place in a half-pint jar. Seal jar.

Attach the following recipe to the jar:

Vanilla Hot Chocolate

1 1/2 cups milk
1/4 cup vanilla hot chocolate mix from jar

Heat the milk in a small saucepan until almost boiling. Add hot chocolate mix and stir until the chocolate is melted. Continue to stir over low heat until hot. Yield: 4 servings.

Candy Cane Hot Chocolate Mix

FILLS ONE QUART GLASS JAR

1 1/2 cups powdered sugar
1 cup + 2 tablespoons cocoa
1 1/2 cups nondairy creamer
4 4-inch peppermint sticks, crushed
Mini marshmallows

Blend together nondairy creamer and peppermint sticks. In a quart jar, layer ingredients in this order: powdered sugar, cocoa, and creamer mixture, packing each layer well. Fill the remaining space in top of jar with a layer of mini marshmallows that have been put in a small resealable plastic bag. Seal jar.

Attach the following recipe to the jar:

Candy Cane Hot Chocolate

Remove marshmallows from jar and set aside. Pour the remaining ingredients from the jar into a large mixing bowl; mix well. Spoon the hot chocolate mixture back into canning jar.

In a cup, add 1/4 cup cocoa mixture to 3/4 cup of boiling water; add marshmallows and stir to blend.

NUTS & SNACKS

Granola Skagit

FILLS 2 QUART GLASS JARS OR 4 PINT JARS

4 cups quick cooking oats
1 cup chopped nuts
1 cup wheat germ
1 cup shredded coconut, cut up, or use flaked coconut
1/3 cup melted margarine
1/3 cup honey

In a bowl, combine the oats, nuts, wheat germ and coconut together. Combine the margarine and honey together, add to the oats mixture; mix well. Spread on baking sheets. Bake at 300 degrees F. for 15 minutes. Stir every 5 minutes.

Add:

1 cup diced prunes
1 cup chopped dates

Roll in powdered sugar before adding to granola so they don't stick together. Store in sealed jars. Use within a few weeks. Yield: 8 cups.

Sugary Cinnamon Pretzels

FILLS 4 QUART GLASS JARS

This coating remains stuck to the pretzels surprisingly well. This will fit in 4 quart jars. Or if you need to pack in 5 jars, use the pint and a half jars (found at Wal-Mart). They are as tall as the quart jars but not as wide and hold a little less.

1 (1 lb.) bag tiny twists pretzels
3/4 cup sugar
3/4 cup vegetable oil
3 teaspoons cinnamon

Line 2 baking sheets with foil. Layer half the pretzels on each baking sheet. In a bowl, combine sugar, oil and cinnamon. Pour the mixture on pretzels, stirring to coat. Bake at 300 degrees F for 25 minutes, stirring once while baking. Allow pretzels to completely cool before packing in 4 quart jars.

Brownie Brickle Bits

FILLS 2 TO 3 QUART GLASS JARS

The secret to making crunchy flat brownie pieces with this recipe is to use a 17" x 11" baking sheet or other large baking sheet. Also non-stick cooking spray with flour works the best so the thin brownies don't stick to the pan.

1/2 cup butter or margarine
1 ounce unsweetened chocolate
1/2 cup sugar
1 egg
1/4 teaspoon vanilla
1/3 cup flour
1/2 cup dark chocolate chips
Non-stick cooking or baking spray

Preheat oven to 375 degrees F. In a large saucepan, melt the butter. Remove from heat and add the unsweetened chocolate. Stir until chocolate is melted.

Stir in the sugar, egg and vanilla. Add the flour and mix well. Lightly coat a 17" x 11" baking sheet with cooking spray. Pour the batter on the baking sheet and spread as evenly as possible. Sprinkle the chocolate chips on top.

Bake for exactly 10 minutes. Cool for 15 minutes, then break brownie brickle into uneven bits and pieces, much like peanut brittle. Fill jars.

Chocolate Caramel Pretzels

FILLS ONE PINT GLASS JAR

15 small square pretzels
15 Hershey's Kisses with Caramel
15 M&M's

Layer the M&M's, then the pretzels and wrapped Hershey's kisses in the jar. Seal jar.

Attach the following recipe to the jar:

Chocolate Caramel Pretzels

Preheat oven to 275 degrees F. Line a baking sheet with foil. Place the pretzels on the foil and center an unwrapped Hershey's Kiss in the center of the pretzel. Bake for 2 minutes at 275 degrees F. Immediately press an M&M in the center of each kiss, pressing down gently so the chocolate kiss spreads out. Refrigerate for 15 minutes until chocolate hardens, then store at room temperature.

Firecrackers

FILLS ONE QUART GLASS JAR

40 saltine crackers
2 teaspoons of your favorite grilling spice
Crushed red pepper flakes
1 (10-ounce) brick Cracker Barrel Extra-sharp Cheddar cheese, shredded

Preheat the oven to 475 degrees F. Arrange the crackers in a single layer, sides touching, in a 10x15-inch cake pan. Sprinkle with the grilling spice, then with as many pepper flakes as you dare. Layer the cheese evenly over the crackers.

Place the pan on the center shelf of the oven. Close the oven door and turn off the oven. Leave in the oven for 4 hours. The heated oven will melt and brown the cheese, creating an even coating of crispy brown. Remove from the oven and let cool. Break apart and place in a quart jar.

Spicy Saltines

FILLS 4 QUART GLASS JARS

1 (16 ounce) box saltine crackers
1 (1 ounce) package ranch dressing mix
1 1/2 cups canola oil
2 tablespoons red pepper flakes
1 tablespoon chili powder
2 - 1 gallon resealable plastic bags

In a bowl, combine the ranch dressing mix, oil, red pepper and chili powder. Add half of the crackers to each plastic bag and pour half the oil mixture over them. Seal the bags filled with air. Toss the crackers in the bag every 5 minutes for an hour. Let the crackers rest overnight or at least for 4 hours before placing them in 4 quart jars. One tube of crackers fits in a quart jar.

Sugar Coated Pecans

FILLS 2 PINT GLASS JARS

2 egg whites
1 tablespoon water
1 teaspoon of vanilla
1 pound pecan halves (3 3/4 cups)
3/4 teaspoon salt
1 cup white sugar
1 teaspoon ground cinnamon

In a medium bowl, whip the egg whites and water together until foamy. Add vanilla. In a separate bowl, mix the salt, sugar and cinnamon together.

Add the pecans to the egg white mix and stir to coat the pecans. Lift the pecans out of the egg white mix with a slotted spoon and mix them in the sugar mixture until well covered. (Or put the sugar mixture in a large Ziploc bag, then add the nuts to coat.) Lay the nuts out on a greased or parchment paper covered baking sheet. Bake at 250 degrees F for 1 hour, stirring every 15 minutes.

Chocolate Covered Raisins

FILLS 2 PINT GLASS JARS

1 cup semi-sweet chocolate chips
1/4 cup dark corn syrup
2 cups raisins
2 tablespoons powdered sugar
1 1/2 teaspoons vanilla extract

Mix together chocolate chips and corn syrup in top of a double boiler; bring water to a boil. Lower heat and cook on low until chocolate chips melt, stirring constantly. Remove from heat, and stir in raisins, powdered sugar and vanilla. Drop by small spoonfuls on waxed paper. Store in refrigerator. Place in jars. Makes about 5-1/2 dozen.

Spiced Pretzels

FILLS 6 QUART GLASS JARS

2 (1 lb.) bags hard pretzels
1 cup canola oil
1 teaspoon garlic salt
1 teaspoon lemon pepper
1 teaspoon dill – or – 1 teaspoon ground cayenne pepper
1 package Hidden Valley® Ranch dressing

Break pretzels in a shallow pan. Mix oil, spices and ranch dressing. Pour over broken pretzels. Bake at 200 degrees for 45 minutes, stirring once halfway through baking. When cool, pack in 6 quart jars.

Roasted Chickpea Snack

FILLS ONE PINT GLASS JAR

1 (15 oz.) can chickpeas
2 tablespoons olive oil
1 tablespoon ground cumin
1 teaspoon garlic powder
1/2 teaspoon chili powder
1/8 teaspoon crushed red pepper
1/8 teaspoon ground black pepper
1/8 teaspoon sea salt

Preheat oven to 350 degrees F. Drain and rinse the chickpeas. In a bowl, combine olive oil, ground cumin, garlic powder, chili powder, crushed red pepper, black pepper and sea salt; whisk until well mixed. Add the chickpeas and stir until well coated. Layer the chickpeas on a baking sheet. Bake at 350 degrees F for 45 minutes, stirring occasionally, until slightly crispy and nicely browned.

Spiced Pumpkin Seeds

FILLS ONE PINT GLASS JAR

1 1/2 tablespoons margarine, melted or olive oil
1/2 teaspoon seasoned salt
1/2 teaspoon salt
1/4 teaspoon garlic powder
2 teaspoons Worcestershire sauce
2 cups whole raw pumpkin seeds

Combine the olive oil or margarine, salt, seasoned salt, garlic powder and Worcestershire sauce. Boil the seeds in water for about 35 minutes. Pat dry and combine them with the margarine mixture. Mix thoroughly and place in in a single layer on one or two baking sheets. Bake at 300 degrees F for 1 hour, stirring occasionally.

Exclusively for *100 MORE Easy Recipes In Jars* readers:

Over 2000 Online Labels and Recipe Cards Available at

www.NorthPoleChristmas.com/jarsbook2.html

Other Books by Bonnie Scott

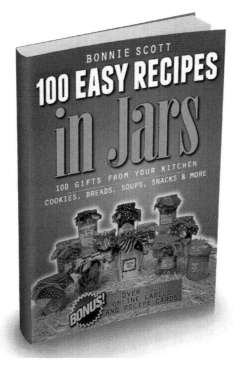

100 Easy Recipes in Jars

Pies and Mini Pies

Holiday Recipes

Simply Fleece

Slow Cooker Comfort Foods

Fish & Game Cookbook

Cookie Indulgence: 150 Easy Cookie Recipes

100 Easy Camping Recipes

Camping Recipes: Foil Packet Cooking

All titles available in Paperback and Kindle versions at Amazon.com

Graphics by Cheryl Seslar

Visit http://www.NorthPoleChristmas.com
for Free Christmas Craft Patterns
and Christmas Printables.

Made in the USA
Middletown, DE
17 February 2016